Street by Street

LUTON
DUNSTABLE

BARTON-LE-CLAY, HARPENDEN, REDBOURN, TODDINGTON

Caddington, Eaton Bray, Edlesborough, Harlington, Hexton, Houghton Regis, Kensworth, Markyate, Stanbridge, Streatley, Totternhoe, Westoning, Whipsnade

3rd edition August 2005
© Automobile Association Developments Limited 2005

Original edition printed May 2001

Ordnance Survey® This product includes map data licensed from Ordnance Survey® with the permission of the Controller of Her Majesty's Stationery Office. © Crown copyright 2005. All rights reserved. Licence number 399221.

Published by AA Publishing (a trading name of Automobile Association Developments Limited, whose registered office (from 1st October 2005) will be Fanum House, Basing View, Basingstoke, Hampshire RG21 4EA. Registered number 1878835).

Mapping produced by the Cartography Department of The Automobile Association. (A02414)

A CIP Catalogue record for this book is available from the British Library.

Printed by GRAFIASA S.A., Porto, Portugal

The contents of this atlas are believed to be correct at the time of the latest revision. However, the publishers cannot be held responsible or liable for any loss or damage occasioned to any person acting or refraining from action as a result of any use or reliance on any material in this atlas, nor for any errors, omissions or changes in such material. This does not affect your statutory rights. The publishers would welcome information to correct any errors or omissions and to keep this atlas up to date. Please write to Publishing, The Automobile Association, Fanum House (FH17), Basing View, Basingstoke, Hampshire, RG21 4EA.

Ref: ML107y

Key to map pages	ii-iii
Key to map symbols	iv-1
Enlarged map pages	2-5
Main map pages	6-73
Index – towns & villages	74
Index – streets	74-80
Index – featured places	80-81
Acknowledgements	81

ii

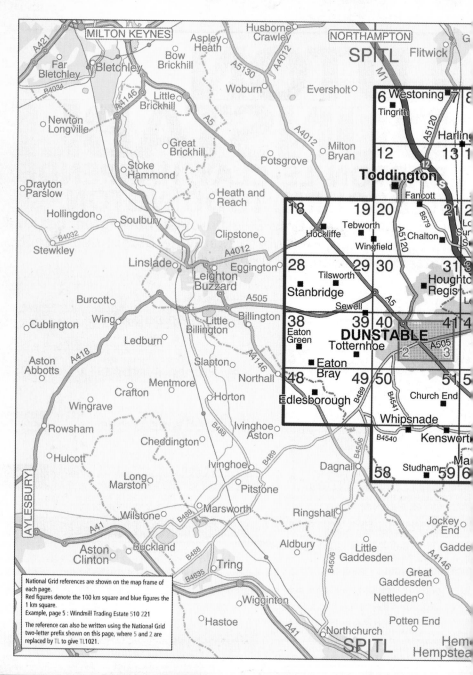

National Grid references are shown on the map frame of each page.
Red figures denote the 100 km square and blue figures the 1 km square.
Example, page 5 : Windmill Trading Estate 510 221

The reference can also be written using the National Grid two-letter prefix shown on this page, where 5 and 2 are replaced by TL to give TL1021.

Scale of enlarged map pages 1:10,000 6.3 inches to 1 mile

miles

kilometres

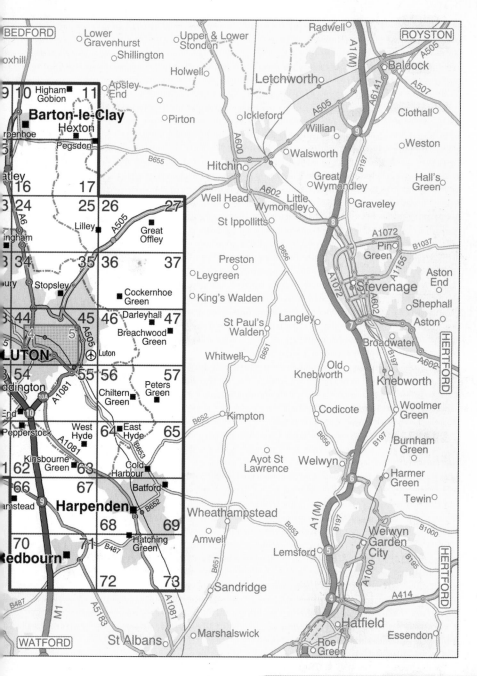

BEDFORD
Lower Gravenhurst
Shillington
oxhill
Apsley End
Higham Gobion
10
9
11
Barton-le-Clay
rpenhoe
Hexton
Pegsdon
atley
16
17
B655
24
25
26
27
Lilley
Great Offley
ingham
A6
A505
34
35
36
37
Stopsley
Cockernhoe Green
ury
44
45
46
Darleyhall
47
Breachwood Green
LUTON
A505
Luton
5
7
4
54
55
56
57
ddington
A1081
Chiltern Green
Peters Green
End
10
Pepperstock
West Hyde
64
East Hyde
65
A1081
B653
Kinsbourne Green
62
63
Cold Harbour
1
66
67
Batford
amstead
9
Harpenden
B652
68
69
70
71
Hatching Green
B487
edbourn
72
73
B487
M1
A5183
A1081
WATFORD
St Albans

Upper & Lower Stondon
Holwell
Pirton
Ickleford
Radwell
Letchworth
ROYSTON
A1(M)
A505
Baldock
A6141
A507
Clothall
9
Weston
Willian
A600
Walsworth
Hitchin
A602
Great Wymondley
Little Wymondley
Graveley
Hall's Green
B197
Well Head
St Ippollitts
8
A1072
Pin Green
B1037
Preston
Leygreen
B656
A1072
A1155
Aston End
King's Walden
Stevenage
Shephall
St Paul's Walden
Langley
7
A602
Aston
Whitwell
B651
Broadwater
B197
A602
Old Knebworth
Knebworth
HERTFORD
B652
Kimpton
Codicote
Woolmer Green
B656
Burnham Green
Ayot St Lawrence
Welwyn
B197
Harmer Green
6
Tewin
Wheathampstead
A1(M)
B197
B1000
Welwyn Garden City
Amwell
B653
Lemsford
5
B195
A1000
HERTFORD
B651
Sandridge
4
A414
Marshalswick
Hatfield
Essendon
Roe Green

4.2 inches to 1 mile   **Scale of main map pages**   1:15,000

0   1/4   miles   1/2   3/4
0   1/4   1/2   kilometres 3/4   1   1 1/4   1 1/2

Junction 9	Motorway & junction
Services	Motorway service area
	Primary road single/dual carriageway
Services	Primary road service area
	A road single/dual carriageway
	B road single/dual carriageway
	Other road single/dual carriageway
	Minor/private road, access may be restricted
← ←	One-way street
	Pedestrian area
	Track or footpath
	Road under construction
	Road tunnel
P	Parking
P+	Park & Ride
	Bus/coach station
	Railway & main railway station
	Railway & minor railway station
⊖	Underground station

⊖	Light railway & station
++++++++++	Preserved private railway
LC	Level crossing
•—•—•—•	Tramway
- - - - - -	Ferry route
....	Airport runway
— · — · — · —	County, administrative boundary
▾▾▾▾▾▾▾▾▾	Mounds
17	Page continuation 1:15,000
3	Page continuation to enlarged scale 1:10,000
	River/canal, lake, pier
	Aqueduct, lock, weir
465 ▲ Winter Hill	Peak (with height in metres)
	Beach
	Woodland
	Park
† † † † †	Cemetery
	Built-up area
	Featured building

⌐⌐⌐⌐⌐⌐⌐	City wall	♜	Castle
A&E	Hospital with 24-hour A&E department	🏛	Historic house or building
PO	Post Office	Wakehurst Place NT	National Trust property
📖	Public library	🏛 M	Museum or art gallery
i	Tourist Information Centre	♞	Roman antiquity
[*i*]	Seasonal Tourist Information Centre	⚱	Ancient site, battlefield or monument
🛢🛢	Petrol station, 24 hour Major suppliers only	🏭	Industrial interest
†	Church/chapel	❀	Garden
🚻	Public toilets	◉	Garden Centre Garden Centre Association Member
♿	Toilet with disabled facilities	🌳	Garden Centre Wyevale Garden Centre
PH	Public house AA recommended	🌲	Arboretum
🍴	Restaurant AA inspected	🛒	Farm or animal centre
Madeira Hotel	Hotel AA inspected	🦌	Zoological or wildlife collection
🎭	Theatre or performing arts centre	🐦	Bird collection
🎥	Cinema	🦆	Nature reserve
⚑	Golf course	◀❙◀	Aquarium
▲	Camping AA inspected	V	Visitor or heritage centre
🚐	Caravan site AA inspected	♔	Country park
▲🚐	Camping & caravan site AA inspected	⌒	Cave
🎡	Theme park	✺	Windmill
🏰	Abbey, cathedral or priory	🛢	Distillery, brewery or vineyard

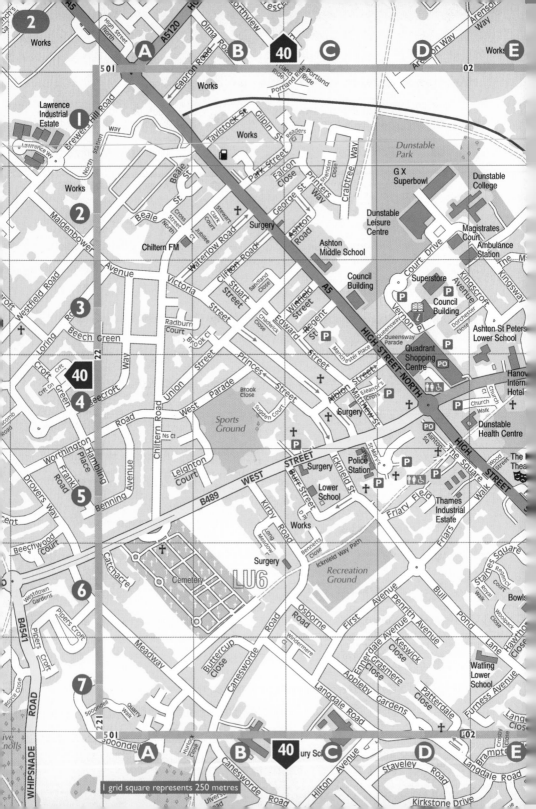

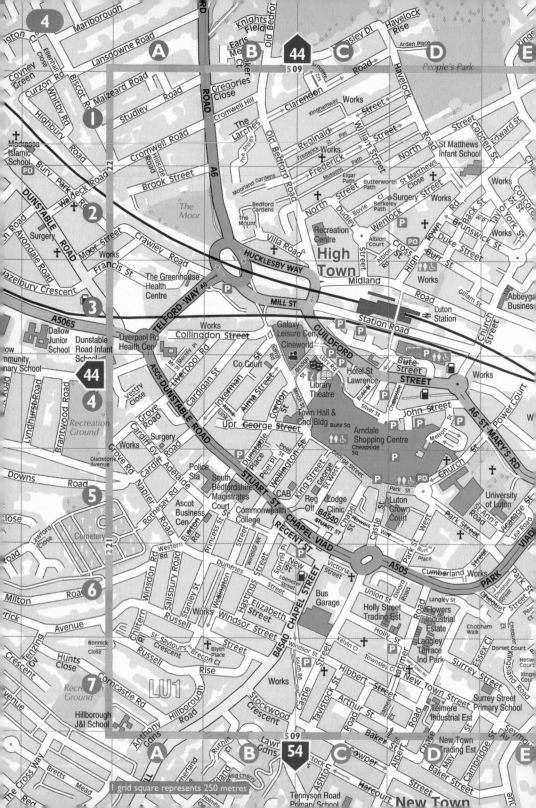

E · F · G · H

Kitchenend Farm

Barton Road

A6

BEDFORD ROAD

33

08

07

1

2

32

Faldo Farm

Faldo Road

Barton Industrial Estate

3

10

Hanover Pl

Stuart Road

Harris Ct

Peck Court

Brazier

Grange Farm Cl

B655

Bedford Road

Birch Rd

Lime

Ash La

Fisher

Grange Rd

Meadhook

Franklin

Mill Lane

Avenue

4

Braziers Cl

Chiltern Road

Brook End Green Farm

A6

Pk Mdw Cl

Longcroft Dr

Brook End Drive

Nicholls Cl

PO

Apple Glebe

Hexton Rd

Horsler Cl

23

5

Rovers FC

Barton Road

Sharpenhoe Road

hoe

Pyghtle School

Priory Farm

E · F · 15 · G · H

07

08

Luton Road

Orchard Close

Washbrook

Orchar

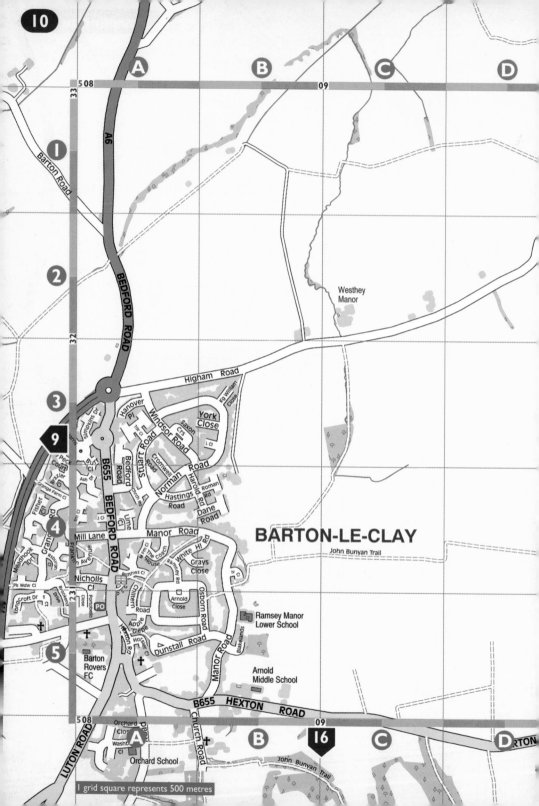

10

A B C D

1 Barton Road

A6

2

BEDFORD ROAD

Westhey Manor

Higham Road

3

9

Hanover Pl
Windsor Road
York Close
Stuart Road
B655
Bedford Road
Cromwell
Norman Road
Harold Rd
Hastings Road
Dane Road
Roman Cl
Peck Court
Grange Farm Cl
Fisher
Ash Cl
Lime Cl
Simkins Dr
Kg William Close
Saxon

4 Mill Lane
Manor Road
Meadbrook
Grancroft
Franklin Avenue
The Coach House
Botshws Cl
White Hl Rd
Grays Close
Ramsey Rd
BEDFORD ROAD
Nicholls Cl
Pk Mdw Cl
Ionacroft Dr
Brookend
Browns Cl
PO
Chiltern Road
Apple Glebe
Ho Clse
Arnold Close
Osborn Road
Blakelands

BARTON-LE-CLAY

John Bunyan Trail

Ramsey Manor
Lower School

5 Barton Rovers FC
Dunstall Road
Hexton Rd

Arnold Middle School

Manor Road

B655 HEXTON ROAD

16

A B C D

LUTON ROAD
Orchard Close
Washbrk Cl
Church Road
Orchard School

John Bunyan Trail

BARTON Rd

1 grid square represents 500 metres

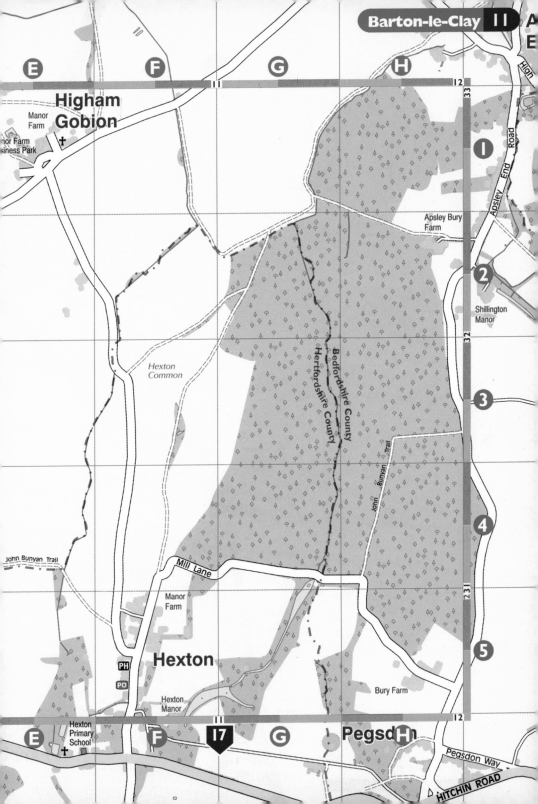

E F G H

Higham Gobion

Manor Farm

nor Farm siness Park

I

Apsley End Road

High

Apsley Bury Farm

2

Shillington Manor

32

3

Hexton Common

Bedfordshire County

Hertfordshire County

John Bunyan Trail

4

John Bunyan Trail

Mill Lane

Manor Farm

231

5

Hexton

PH

PO

Bury Farm

Hexton Manor

12

E F **17** G **Pegsdon**

Hexton Primary School

Pegsdon Way

HITCHIN ROAD

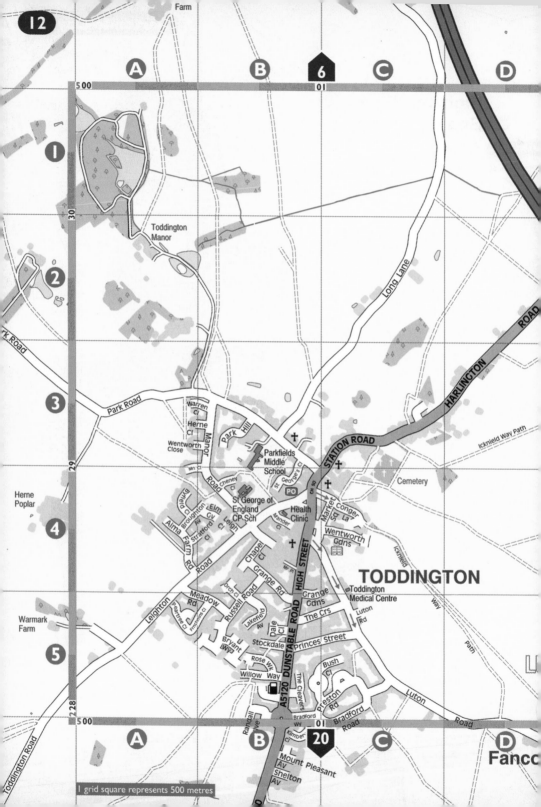

Farm

A　　　　B　　6　　C　　　　D

5 00　　　　　　01

1

30

Toddington
Manor

2

Park Road

Herne
Poplar

3　　Park Road

Warren
Cl

Herne
Cl

Wentworth
Close

Manor Road

Park Hill

Parkfields
Middle
School

St George's

cheney Cl

St Geo Cl

Long Lane

HARLINGTON ROAD

STATION ROAD

Icknield Way Path

Cemetery

29

4

Alma Farm Rd

Broughton Av

Elm Gv

Stratford Cl

Leigh Cl

St George of
England CP Sch

Mander Cl

PO

Health
Clinic

Market Sq

Conger La

Wentworth
Gdns

Icknield

TODDINGTON

Toddington
Medical Centre

Way

Warmark
Farm

5

Leighton Road

Meadow
Rd

Bran Cl

Pear tree Cl

Periwinkle Cl

Chapel Cl

Grange Rd

Russell Road

Lakefield
Av

Dale Cl

HIGH STREET

Grange
Gdns

The Crs

Luton
Rd

Way

Path

L

Bryant
Wy

Stockdale

Rose Wk

Willow Way

A5120

DUNSTABLE ROAD

Princes Street

Bush
Cl

The Cleavers

Randall
Dve

Bradford
Wy

Preston
Rd

Bradford

Luton

Road

2 28

5 00

01

A　　　　B　　20　　C　　　　D

Kimber
Cl

Mount Pleasant
Av
Shelton
Av

Fancc

Toddington Road

Toddington **13**

Redhills Farm

E **F** **7** Toddington **G** Road **H** Cemetery

PO Brian Way

Barton Road

03 Station Road

Manor Close

Surgery

Harlington

I

Harlington Station

Christian Close

Prudence Close

Pilgrims Close

Park Leys

St Cl

Valiant Close

Bury Close

Wood F

2 Sundon

30

A5120 HARLINGTON ROAD

Garden Centre

Junction 12

Old Park Farm

Dyer's Hall Farm

Icknield Way Path

3

14

29

4

Icknield Way Path

M1

Toddington Service Area

Travelodge

Cowbridge Farm

5

228

E **F** **21** **G** **H** **Upper Sund**

03 04

14

Lincoln Way
Brian Road
Barton Road
Church Road
Cemetery
PO
East End Farms

A 504 **B** **8** 05 **C** **D**

Harlington

1

Bury Close

30

2

Wood Farm

Sundon Road

Dyer's Hall Farm

3

Sundon Road

13

29

Sundon Hills Country Park

4

Icknield Way Path

Icknield Way Path

Harlington Road

Icknield Way Path

Icknield Way Path

Holtwood Farm

5

228

504 05

A **B** **22** **C** **D**

Upper Sundon

PO

Harlington Rd

Sundon Lower School

Deatley Road

I grid square represents 500 metres

Rovers FC

Barton Road

Sharpenhoe Road

nhoe

E

ghtle School

F

9

07

G

H

08

LUTON ROAD

Orchard Close
Washbrook Cl
Orch

Priory Farm

I

Moleskin

30

2

Sharpenhoe Road

John Bunyan Trail

Icknield Way Path

A6

Bartonhill Cutting

3

16

29

Icknield Way Pth

John Bunyan Trail

LUTON ROAD

4

Church Road

A6

St Margarets Cl

Churchill Cl

Stanley Rd

5

Sundon Road

Streatley

Streatley Road

Bury La

Sharpenhoe Road

LUTON ROAD A6

228

E

F

07

23

G

H

08

Sharpenhoe Rd

Icknield Way Path

16

Barton
Rovers
FC

Dunstall Road

Manor Road

Arnold
Middle School

A B655 HEXTON ROAD **B** **10** 09 **C** **D**

5 08

BARTON

LUTON ROAD

Orchard
Close
Washbrook
Cl
Orchard School

Old Road

Church Road

Cemetery

John Bunyan Trail

1

30

2

Barton Hills
Nature Reserve

Ravensburgh
Castle ⚔

Jeremiah's
Tree

artonhill
utting

3

John Bunyan Trail

15

29

4

Barton
Hill Farm

5

John Bunyan Trail

2 28

5 08

09

nhoe

Icknield Way Path **A** **B** **24** **C** **D**

Hertfordshire County
Bedfordshire County

I grid square represents 500 metres

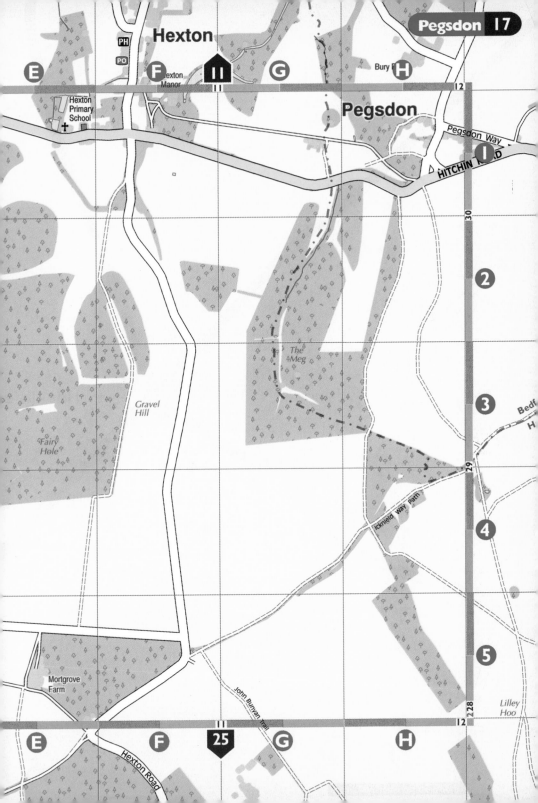

E F G H
99 500 28

I

2

Chalgrave

27

3

20

Tebworth

Toddington Road

The Lane

PO

Works

Parkview Lane

St Mary's
Close

Woodlands

Wingfield Road

Hockliffe Road

Tebworth Road

4
...worth

Wing...

Hill Cl

226

Hill
Farm

Icknield Way Path

5

Farm

Trinity
Hall

99 500

E F **29** G H

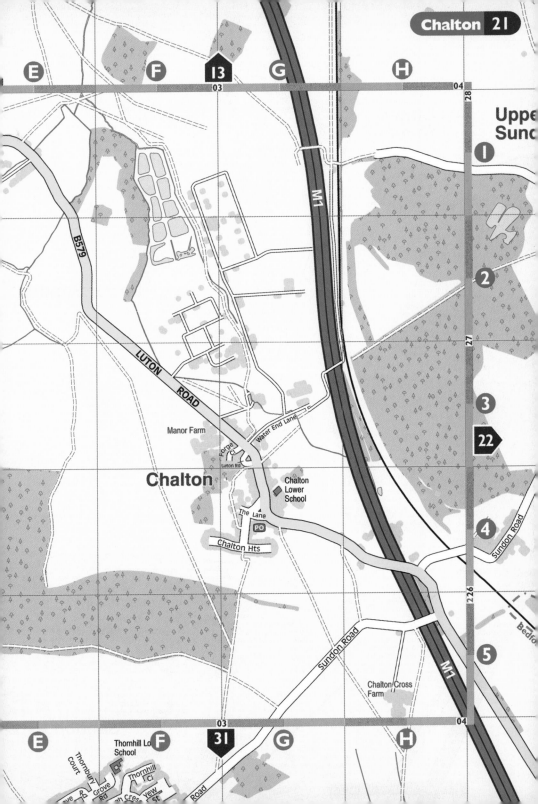

E F **13** G H

03 · 04 · 28

I

2

27

3

22

4

226

5

Upper
Sund

B579

LUTON ROAD

Manor Farm

Water End Lane

Forge Cl

Luton Rd

Chalton

Chalton Lower School

The Lane

PO

Chalton Hts

M1

Sundon Road

Sundon Road

Bedfor

Chalton Cross Farm

E F **31** G H

03 · 04

Thornhill Lo School

Thornbury Court

Thornhill Cl

Grove Rd

Yew St

Road

A B 16 C D

508
28
Icknield Way Path

Herifordshire County
Bedfordshire County

BARTON

I

New
Farm

2

ROAD
27

Icknield Way Path

3

John Bunyan Trail

John Buny 23

Golf Course

South Bedfordshire
Golf Club

John Bunyan Trail

Icknield Way Path

Turnpike Dr

Turnpike
Dr

BARTON ROAD

Turnpike
Dr

Quantock Rise
Milburn Cl
Statham
Close
Ewington Gdns
Chard Drive
Scombe

4

Cardinal
Newman
School

Icknield Way Path

Barnfield Coll
Technology Cen

Bramingham
Business
Park

Whitwell Cl

5

Superstore

Warden Hill Rd

Warden Hi

Way

Markham
Rd
Wycombe Wy

Hillcrest
Av

Icknield Way Path

508
09

A B 34 C D

Cromer

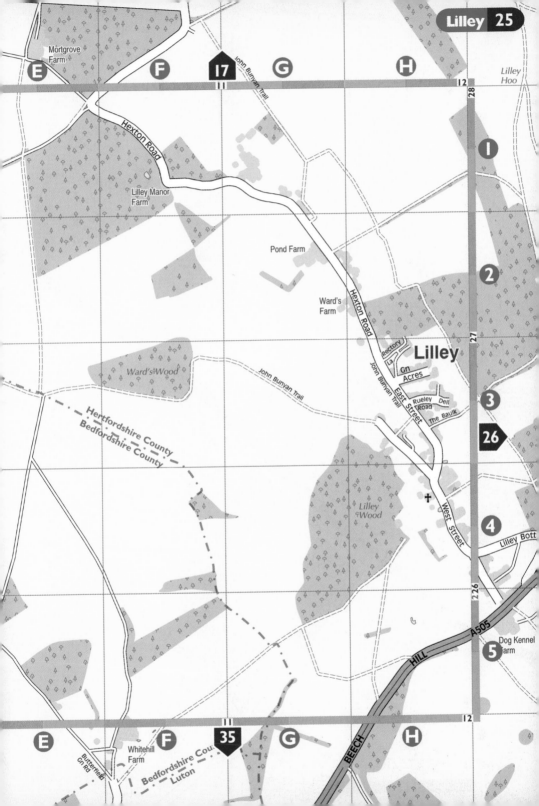

Mortgrove Farm

E   F   **17**   G   H

Lilley Hoo

John Bunyan Trail

12   28

Hexton Road

I

Lilley Manor Farm

Pond Farm

2

Hexton Road

Ward's Farm

27

Lilley

Rectory La
Gn Acres

John Bunyan Trail

Ward's Wood

John Bunyan Trail

Rueley Road   Dell

3

East Street

The Baulk

Hertfordshire County
Bedfordshire County

26

†

Lilley Wood

West Street

4

Lilley Bott

226

A505

BEECH

HILL

Dog Kennel Farm

5

12

E   F   **35**   G   H

Butterfield Gn Rd

Whitehill Farm

Bedfordshire Cou
Luton

26

Ⓐ Ⓑ Ⓒ Ⓓ

Lilley Hoo
5|12
28
|3

I

Cloudshill

Wester

2

A505

Lilley Hoo
Farm

Lilley

27

Acres

Lilleyhoo Lane

Rueley
Road

Luton Road

3

The Bauik

Street

Hollybush Hill

25

Luton White Hill

✝

Wes

4

eet

Lilley Bottom

2 26

Luton White Hill

A505

5

Dog Kennel
Farm

West
Wood

HILL

5|12

Ⓐ Ⓑ Ⓒ Ⓓ
|3

36

Lilley

1 grid square represents 500 metres

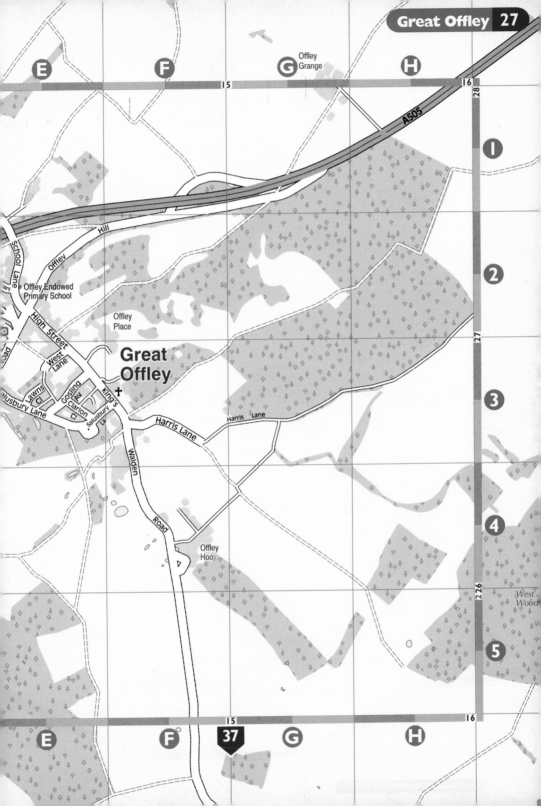

E F G H

Offley Grange

A505

15 16

28

1

2

27

3

Offley Hill

School Lane

Offley

Offley Endowed
Primary School

High Street

Offley Place

Great Offley

West Lane

Lawns Cl

Salusbury Lane

Gosling Av

Clarion Cl

King's La

Salusbury La

Harris Lane

Harris Lane

Walden

Road

Offley Hoo

4

226

West Wood

5

E F **37** G H

15 16

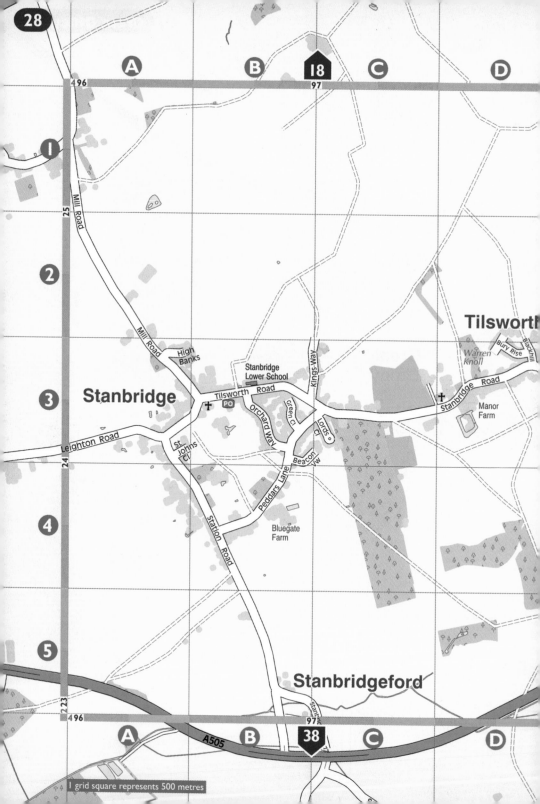

28

A B **18** C D

496 97

1

25 Mill Road

2

Mill Road

High Banks

Stanbridge Lower School

Kings Way

Tilsworth

Warren Knoll

Bury Rise

Blackhill

3 **Stanbridge**

Tilsworth Road

PO

Orchard Way

Green Cl

Lords Cl

Stanbridge Road

Manor Farm

Leighton Road

24

St Johns Cl

Beacon Vw

4

Station Road

Peddars Lane

Bluegate Farm

5

2 23

496

Stanbridgeford

Stanbr

A B **38** C D

A505 97

1 grid square represents 500 metres

E

F Trinity Hall

19
99

G

H

500

I

25

Thorn

2

Tilsworth Golf Centre

Dunstable Road

Golf Course

A5

Tho

3

30

24

kens La

ry rm

Icknield Way Path

4

Chalk

A505

Sewell Lane

5

Sewell Lane

223

E

F

99

39

G

500

Sev H ll

Sundon Road

Chalton Cross
Farm

E   F   21   G   H

M1

03   04

I

25

2

3

32

Thornhill Lower
School

Thornhill Court

Grove Rd
Grove Rd
Thornhill Cl

Grove Rd
Grove Rd
Hillborough Crescent
Yew St

Eddiwick Av
Kent Road

Sundon Road

Kings Houghton
Middle School

Kingsland
Community
College

Tithe
Farm

PO

Road

Sycamore Road

Recreation Rd

Westminster Gdns

Elm Pk Cl

Parkside Drive

Brentwood

Enfield Cl

Abbey Walk
Maple Way
Rose Walk
Therfield Walk
Ashwell Walk

Houghton Park Rd

Minton Walk

Newbury Rd

Trident Drive

Dolphin Drive

Chelsea Gdns

Hawthorn Park
Lower School

Bromley Gardens

Parkside Drive

Cumbria Cl

Fenwick Rd

Conquest Rd

Parkside Drive

Fensome Dr

Henley

Rosedale

Conway

Hammersmith Gdns

Lower School

Parkside

Turner
Vanbrugh
Nash Cl
Constable Cl

Bridgeman

Bloomsbury Gdns

Lowry Drive
Chapin
Stubbs

Houghton Regis

Windsor Dr

Parkside Cl

Crossways

The Green

East End

Woodlands Av

Moore Crs

Brookfield

Loughbrooke

Halley's Wy

Windsor

Tennyson Av

Milton Wy

North Road

Houghton Hall

Kingsland Cl

Copperfield

Tudor Drive

Kensington

Sandringham Dr

Evans Cl

Surgery

Thresher

Paddock Cl

Gelding Cl

Pastures Wy

Buzzard

Peregrine Road

Lapwing
Bunting
Swallow
Skua

Pastures

Road

St Kilda Rd

Radnor Road

Oakfield

Sussex Cl

Wedgewood Rd

Chantry J&I
School

Southfi
J&I School

4

Santon

Clover

Wheatfield

Reaper

Plough

Binder

Landrace Road

Haymarket Rd

Thatch

Tomlinson Road

PO

Beadlow Road

Purcell Rd

Trefoil

Friesian Cl

Drayton

Porz Avenue

Humphrys Road

Road

Martins

Regis Road

Cedar Cl

Aspley Cl

Carfax

Brunel

Kimberley

Aberdeen

Acorn

Brunel Cl

Lewsey
Farm

Baldock

Ramsey

Jersey Rd

Percheron

5

Woodside Park
Industrial Estate

Woodside
Industrial
Estate

Lovett Way

Verey Rd

Apex
Business
Centre

E

Eyncourt Road

Buscombe Road

Works

F   41   G   H

03   04

Poynters Road

Wilbury Drive

Mill Vale
Middle
School

Holmwood Close

Goldstone Crs

Hadrian

Duncombe

Holliwick Road

Lockington Crs

Millers

Markham Crs

Emerald Rd

Jillifer Road

Wimpole

Browning Rd

Marlin Rd

Belsize Rd

Kirkwood Road

Aberdeen

Braintree

Rodney Cl

Amhurst Rd

Leagrave

High Street

Halyard
High School

Old
Dairy Court

Evelyn

Poynters Road

Avenue

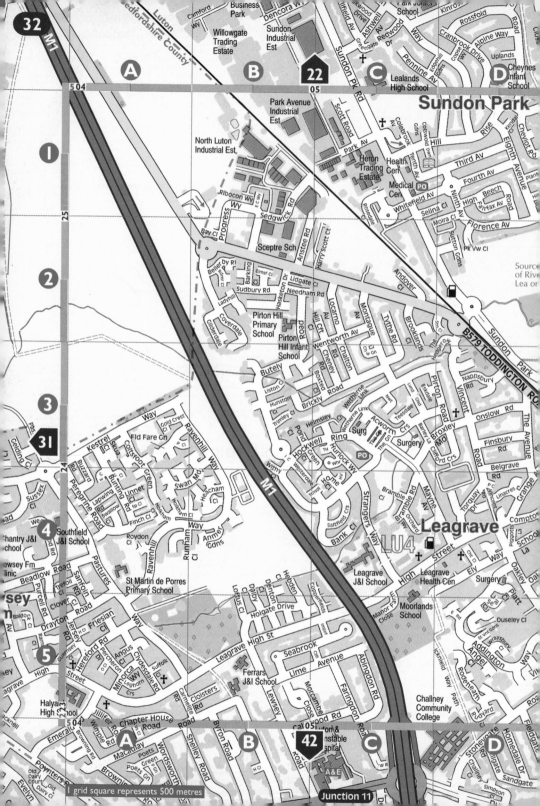

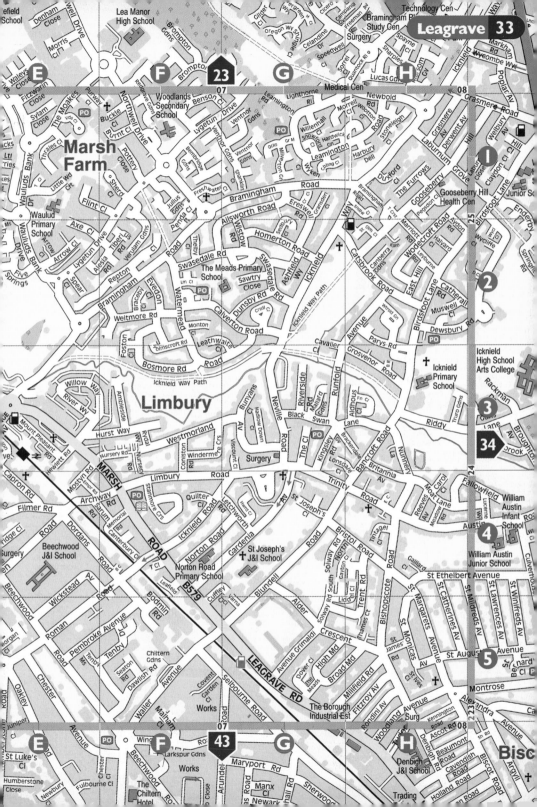

A505

BEECH HI

Stopsley Hi

E F 25 G H 12

I

25

Bedfordshire County
Luton

Whitehill
Farm

Butterfield
Gn Rd

Butterfield
Green

Butterfield
Green

Hitchin Rd

The Vale
Crematorium

The Vale
Cemetery

Manor
Farm

HITCHIN ROAD A505

Putteridge
Bury

2

University
of Luton

Wren Close

Edgewood Drive

Nightingale

Jaywood

Curlew

Corncrake

Mount Grace

Swifts Green Road

Wood Gn

Swifts Gn

Wood Green Road

Ravenbank Road

Close

Crowland Road

Putteridge
High School

Putteridge Rd

3

36

Putteridge
J&I School

Recreation
Centre

Rogate Rd

Birling

Bkgry Cl

Bicmb Cl

Pvns Cl

Ambr Cl

Selsey Drive

F E C

Mdsf Rd

24

4
Cockernh
Green

ley Sports Centre
rts Ground

Greenways

Cannon Lane

Hayes Road

Road

Rd

Rochester

Westway

Lotnair Road

Venetia
Rd

Tant Cl Red

Mullion
Cl

Delicot
Cl

B Cl

Putteridge

Clingrr

Stapleford Road

Chesford

Briar
Cl

Blackthorn

Wandon
Close

Eastfield

Chesford

Way

Hawthorn Avenue

Applecroft
Rd

Mayfield Rd

Dr

Bracklesham

St Tths Cl

PO

Surgery

Hazelwood
Close

Ravensthorpe

Peartree Road

Green Lane

Telscombe

Cl

Satndean

5

Ch Cl Cl

Stopsley
Primary
School

A505 Road

Walnut
Cl

Ashcroft Rd

Dahlia
Cl

Wigmore

Poplars
Cl

Sowerby Av

Telscombe
Way

Hayling Drive

Ilford

Tilgate

Nymans

Copthorne

Elmtr

Hitchin

Stopsley Way

Forrest Crs

Surgery

PO

Brays Road

Hallwicks Rd

Mobley
Ln Cl

Alfriston
Close

Cullington Cl

Seaford Cl

Dinchms

Rother

Slaughter's
Wood

Sacred Heart
J&I School

Shelton
Way

Arnold
Cl

Landford Drive

Stephens Cl

Turners Rd

North

Lady Zia
Werner Sch

O'onnell Cl

Sibley Cl

Rck Cl Cl

Church Rd

Garretts Md

Long
Lane

Mangrove Rd

Somereies
J&I School

Horsham Rd

STOPSLEY WAY

A50

Deep
Denes

Kynance Cl

stephens
Gardens

Moreton

Moreton
Rd s

E F 45 G H

Moreton Park
Industrial Estate

Clevedon Road

Ramridge
Primary School

Hanswick
Close

Ashcroft Rd

Marshall
Md

Styles

Keepers

Chalfont Rd

Wigmore Road

Buckingham Drive

Buckingh

Bexhill Rd

Kempsey Cl

Astley

Claverley Gn

Green Road

Rochford Drive

B Cl

LU2

E F **27** G H

15 16

I

25

Stopsley Holes
Farm

2

Kingswell
End

**Ley
Green**

Plough Lane

Lodge
Farm

3

24

Stony Lane

4

Church Road

Lilley

Church Road

Bottom

**King's
Walden**

5

Lilley

223

Windmill Road

15 16

E **F** **47** G H

Windmill Road

Bottom

Road

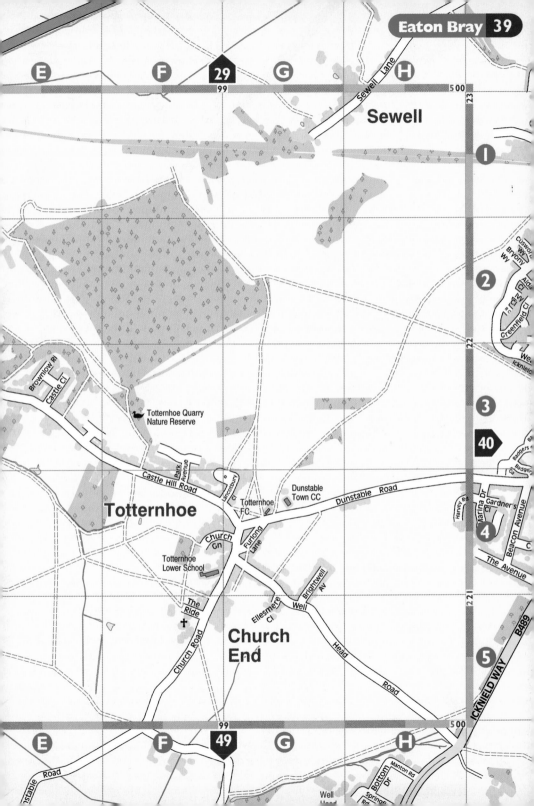

E   F   **29**   G   H

99   5 00   23

Sewell

Sewell Lane

I

2

Cusworth Wy
Bryony Wy
Aldeburgh Cl
Greenfield Cl
West Icknield

22

3

Brownlow Rl
Castle Cl

Totternhoe Quarry
Nature Reserve

40

Badgers Cl
Badgers Cl

Park Avenue

Castle Hill Road

Lancotbury Cl

Totternhoe
FC

Dunstable
Town CC

Dunstable Road

Harvey Rd
Marina Dr
Gardner's Cl
Beacon Avenue
C

4

Totternhoe

Church
Gn

Furlong Lane

The Avenue

221

Totternhoe
Lower School

The
Ride

Church Road

Ellesmere Cl

Well

Brightwell Av

Head

Road

ICKNIELD WAY
B489

5

**Church
End**

99   5 00

E   F   **49**   G   H

stable Road

Bottom Dr

Manton Rd

Springs Rd

Well
Head

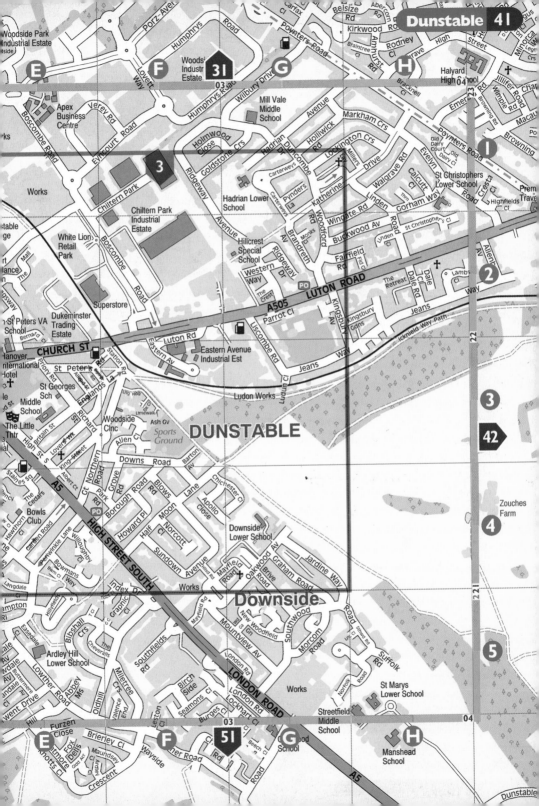

Walden

E F **37** G Lilley H

Windmill Road

15 23

Bottom

I

Windmill Road

Millway

The Heath

Darley Road

Road

Lower

2

Darleyhall

Heath Road

St Mary's Rise

22

Colemans Road

Orchard Way

The Mdw

Chapel Road

Oxford Rd

Breachwood Green Primary School

PO †

Breachwood Green

Bailey's Farm

3

Gro Farm

Pasture

Lane

4

Lye Hill

Long

Whiteway Bottom

221

Diamond End

5

16

Whitewaybottom

Wandon Green Farm

E F **57** G Lane H

Lawren

15 16

48

A · **496** · B · **38** · **97** · C · D

Eaton Bray Lower School

Eaton Bray

Wallace Dr

The Nurser

Saffron Rd

Wivesfield

Church La

High Street

School Lane

Gurney Ct

Eaton Pk

PO

Medley Close

The Meads

Church La

Perry Md

Knights Cl

Bower Lane

Moor End

Yew Tree Cl

The Chrs

Orchard Wk

Moor End

Mill End

Close

Waterside

PO

Summerleys

Cow Lane

Broomstick Industrial Est.

Good Intent

Orchard End

Jacksons Ct

Brook Street

Tasker's Row

Surgery

Tasker's Row

Wren Wk

The Green

Slicke

Edlesborough

Cook's Meadow

St Mary Cl

High Street

Kings Mead

Brownlow Avenue

Swann

The Willows

Edlesborough School

Pebblemoor

Townside

Church Croft

Chiltern Avenue

Eaton Bray Road

Northall Road

The Sears

The Pepplatts

Beacon View

South End Lane

A4146

LEIGHTON ROAD

I

2

3

4

5

20

19

218

A4146

LEIGHTON ROAD

Ivinghoe Way

496 · **97**

A · **Coombe Bottom** · B · C · **Pine Road** · D

Travellers Rest

1 grid square represents 500 metres

E   F   39   G   H

Church Road

Head

Road

ICKNIELD WA

99

500

I

Dunstable Road

Doolittle
Mill

Well
Head

Manton Rd

Bottom
Dr

Springfield
Rd

B489

20

Harling Road

Icknield Way
Farm

2

Harling Road

3

50

19

LU6

4

WAY

Valance-end
Farm

DAGNALL

B4540

5

ICKNIELD

ROAD

B4506

B489

ICKNIELD

B4540

218

99

500

E   F   G   H

Willow
Farm

Buck

Bed

Avenue

Dukes Avenue

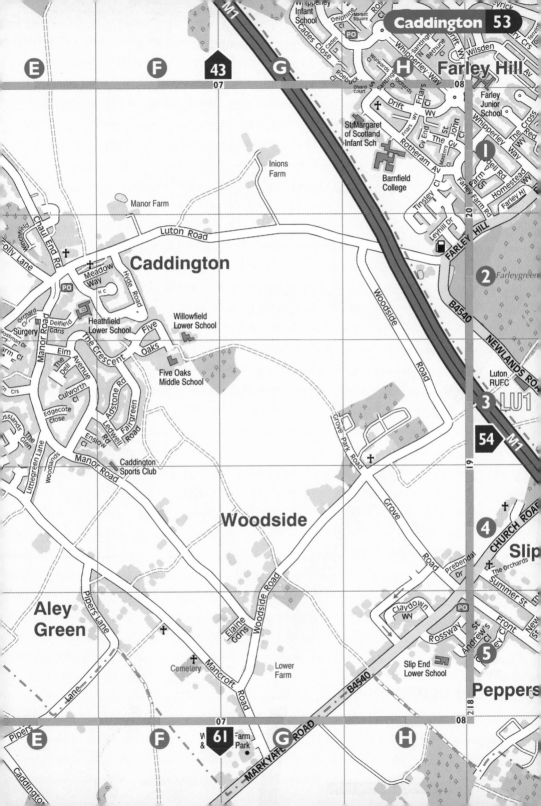

Farley Hill

M1

Whipperley Infant School

Cades Close

Delphine Cl

Market Square

PO

Olyard Court

Yrick

Trift Crs

Wilsden

Santingfield

Bethune

Whipperley Way

Wulwards

Richards

Drift

Friars Wy

St John

GV

Farley Junior School

Red Cross

The Croft

Av

Roebuck

Roos

Santin

E **F** **43** **G** **H**

07 08

St Margaret of Scotland Infant Sch

Rotheram Av

Friars Ct End

St John GV

Masters Cl

Bell Rd

Farley Farm Rd

Homestead Wy

Farley Hl

I

Inions Farm

Barnfield College

Tinsley Cl

20

Leyhill Dr

FARLEY HILL

Manor Farm

Luton Road

Caddington

Woodside Road

2 Farleygreen

B4540

Meadow Way

PO

H C

Hyde Road

Willowfield Lower School

3 **LU1**

NEWLANDS ROAD

Luton RUFC

Orchard Cl

Surgery

Crossman Dr

Farm Cl

Delfield Gdns

Heathfield Lower School

Five Oaks

Five Oaks Middle School

19

Elm Dell

The Dell

Manor Road

Avenue

The Crescent

Culworth Cl

Adstone Rd

Fairgreen

Ledwell Rd

Fairgreen Road

Grove Park Road

54 **M1**

Edgecote Close

Enslow Cl

4 **CHURCH ROAD**

Slip

Rosslands The Glen

Littlegreen Lane

Woodlands

Manor Road

Caddington Sports Club

Woodside

Grove Road

Prebendal Dr

The Orchards

Summer St

Claydown Wy

PO

St Andrew's CE

New

Front

5

Aley Green

Pipers Lane

Elaine Gdns

Woodside Road

Mancroft Road

Lower Farm

Rossway

Slip End Lower School

Peppers

Cemetery

B4540

21B

Pipers

Lane

E **F** **61** **G** **H**

07 08

Caddington

W & Farm Park

MARKYATE ROAD

Luton
Retail Park

P

A505 GIPSY LANE

E **P**

Luton Airport
Parkway Station

F

Vauxhall
Road

45

Barratt
Ind Park

G

H

Airport

P

AIRPORT WAY

A505

LOWER HARPENDEN
ROAD

AIRPORT

Upper Lea valley Walk

Lea Valley Walk

Somerles

I

12

Somerles Castle

Someries Castle

20

The
Luton Dr

Luton Drive

**er Kidney
od**

Bush
Pasture

2

The

George
Wood

3

56

19

Luton Hoo
Park

River Lea or Lee

4

Lea Valley Walk

5

The Warren Drive

Birch
Wood

E

Home Farm

F

63

G

H

218

B653

Low

12

**New
Mill End**

56

Luton

Bedfordshire County

A   B   **46**   Dane Street Farm   C   D

5|2 |3

Chiltern Hall

Hertfordshire County
Bedfordshire County

Withstock's Wood

Someries

1

Someries Castle

20

Copt Hall

2

George Wood

3

55

19

Chiltern
Green

4

Lea Valley Walk

5

2|8

B653

5|2 |3

New
Mill End

A   WER HARPE   B   **64**   C   D

Farr's Lane

East

1 grid square represents 500 metres

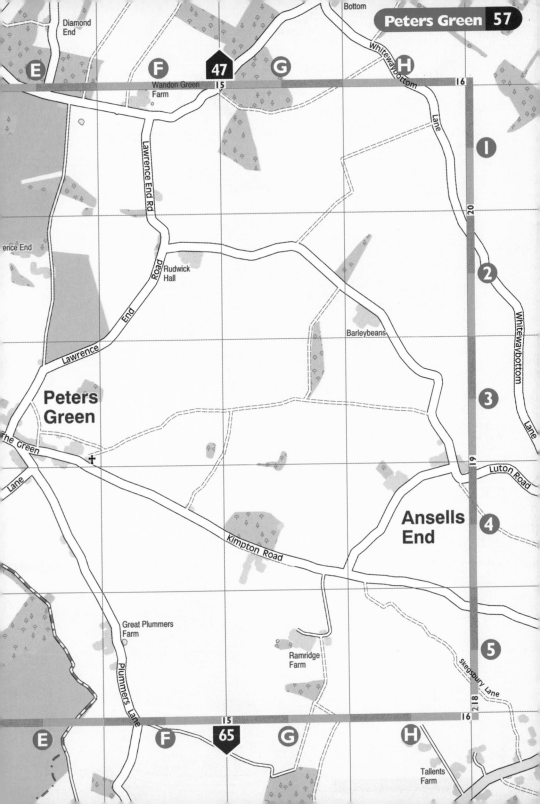

Diamond End

Bottom

Whitewaybottom

E

F

47

G

H

Wandon Green Farm

15

16

I

Lawrence End Rd

20

Whitewaybottom Lane

Road

Rudwick Hall

2

End

Barleybeans

rence End

3

Lawrence

19

Luton Road

Peters Green

The Green

✝

Ansells End

4

Lane

Kimpton Road

Great Plummers Farm

Ramridge Farm

5

Skegsbury Lane

Plummers Lane

218

15

16

E

F

65

G

H

Tallents Farm

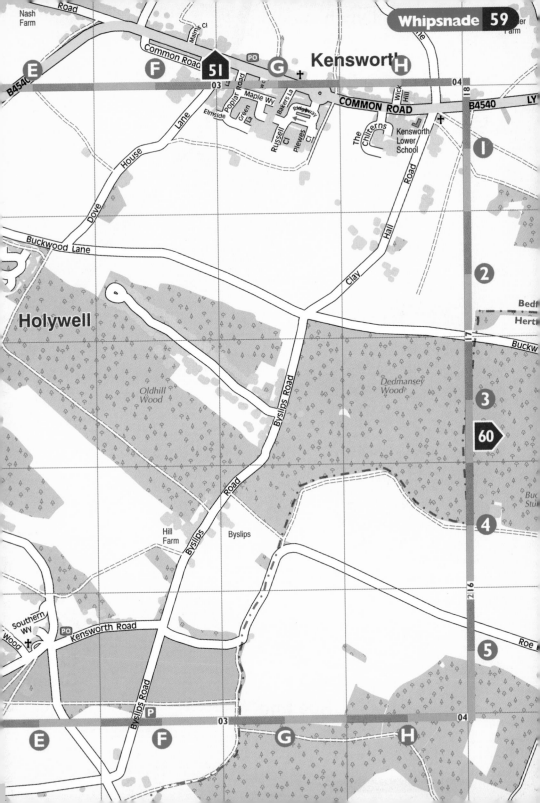

Road

Nash
Farm

Common Road

E

B454C

51

03

PO

Maim's Cl

Elmside

Poplar Road

Green

Maple Wy

Russell
Cl

Bakers La

Plewes
Cl

Ridgeway

House

Lane

Dove

Buckwood Lane

Holywell

Oldhill
Wood

Byslips Road

Hill
Farm

Byslips
Road

Byslips

Road

Southern
Wy

PO

Wood

Kensworth Road

Byslips Road

P

03

E

F

G

G

Kensworth

H

COMMON ROAD

B4540

04

LY

18

The Chilterns

Kensworth
Lower
School

Hall

Clay

Road

I

2

Bedf

Hert

Buckw

Dedmansey
Wood

3

60

Buc
Stu

4

216

Roe

5

04

F

G

H

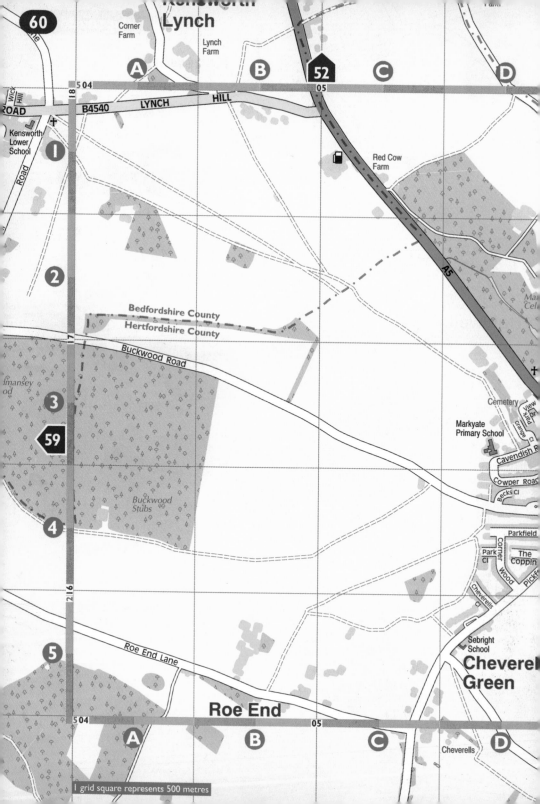

62
Slip End
Lower School

Pepperstock

Andrew Cl
Crawley
Street
ROSS W

Half Moon Lane

B

54

C

D

London Road

Bedfordshire County
Hertfordshire County

1

18
5 08
09

A

Pepsal End
Road

Pepsal
End

2

17

Pepsal End Road

Bonners

3

61

Brae

Gibraltar
Farm

Chad
Lane

4

216

Lady Bray
Farm

5

M1

Watery Lane

Annables

Hill & Coles
Farm

Turner's Hall
Farm

5 08
09

A

B

66

C

D

River Hall

Friar's
Wash

Street

Lane

1 grid square represents 500 metres

E F 55 G **Birch Wood** H

New Mill End

B653 LOW

Home Farm

12 18

1

West Hyde

Farm Road

2

7

Lady Bute's Lodge

Avenue

Limetree

LONDON ROAD

3

64

Thrales

Kennel

Lane

4

Thrales End

Kinsbourne Green

Annables Farm

Chamberlaines

Spring Road

The Common

PO

Derwent Road

Kinsbourne Cl

Tintern Cl

Crosspaths

Greatfield

Tuffnells

Tuffnells Way

Kinsbourne Way

The Close

The Pleasance

K Cl's

Shpr Wy

Crpndrs Cl

Vale Cl

Farm Av

Pnshrs

Molescroft

Way

Luton Rd

5

Ridge Avenue

Ridgewood Drive

Wells Cl

Mayfield Cl

High

Rdg

2 16

12

E F 67 G

Kirne Green La

Wood End School

Ynm Av

Wood End Hl

Wood End Road

H

Ashley Gdns

Haslingden

Brackendale

Roundwood Lane

Woodland

Applewood

How

Rou

Faulkners

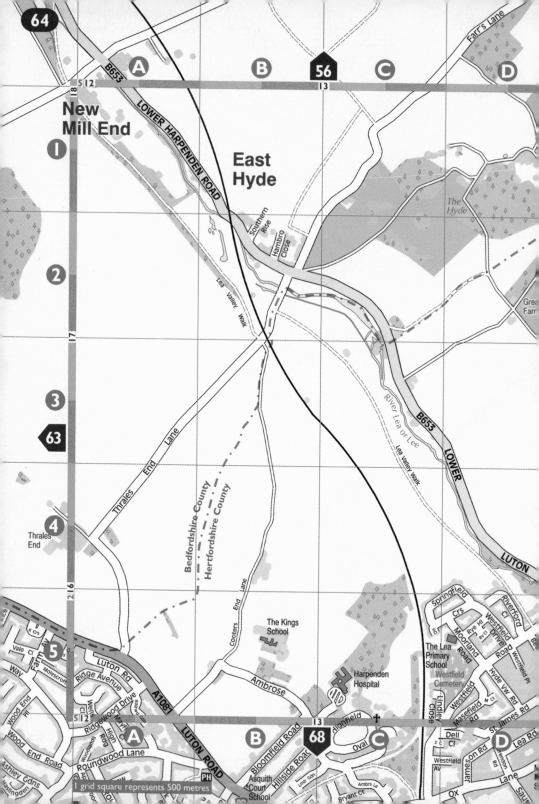

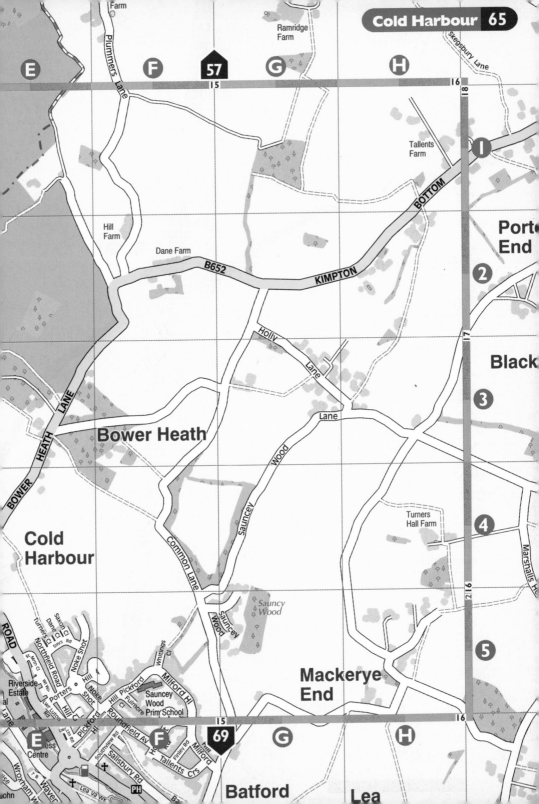

A | **B** | **C** | **D**

5 08

Hill & Coles Farm

62

09

Turner's Hall Farm

Watery Lane

1

River Hall

River Ver

Friar's Wash

A5

Hill

Watery Lane

Junction 9

2

Priory orch

PO

High St

Chequers Hill

Flamstead

Chapel Rd

Trowley Hill Rd

Church Rd

Singlets Lane

Cemetery

Pie Cnr

College Cl

Pie Garden

Herts County Agricultural Showground

A5183

DUNSTABLE ROAD

Vicarage Gdns

's Close

3

Flamstead School

Delmerend Farm

Delmerend Lane

Norringtonend Farm

Redding Lane

Hill Road

Linnins Pond

Trowley Bottom

4

St Agnell's Farm

M1

5

Lybury Lane

2 13

5 08

A | **B** | **C** | **D**

09

70

Nicholls Farm

1 grid square represents 500 metres

Mackerye End

Batford

Lea Valley

Leasey Bridge

Riverside Estate

Allied Business Centre

Crabtree J&I School

Aldwickbury Park Golf Club

Golf Course

Wheathampstead Road

High Beeches Prim Sch

The Grove Junior School

The Grove Infant School

The Grove

Pipers Lane

Southdown Industrial Estate

Eastmoor Park

Cross Farm

Fulmore Prim School

Manor Road

Marshalls Way
Lwr Luton Rd

E   **F**   65   **G**   **H**   **I**

2

3

4

5

E   **F**   73   **G**   **H**

70

A B 66 C D

Nicholls Farm

Tassell Hall

Police Stati...

...nlane

Flamsteadbury Farm

AL3

Lane

Gaddesden Lane

Holtsmere End

Holtsmere End

Great Revel End Farm

Aubrey Lane

ROAD

B48

HEMPSTEAD

Nicky Line

Little Revel End

...mere End Lane

...air Ct

Valley Green

Road

Surgery

PO

Primary School

1 grid square represents 500 metres

HEMEL

Nicky Line

M1

E
F
69
G
H

Southdown Rd

Grove
Longfield Road
King Cft Road
Knowle Dr
Field Cl
Oakle
Road

Vallance
Place
Dicks Fld

Coleswood Road
Tarrant Dr

Thorn La
Sibley Aven
Paddock Wood

Pipers Lane

15

13

Broadstone Park
Eastcote Dr
Rise
Barrons Rw
Enn Cl
Hdlg Ct
Cross Farm

Ayres

Eastmoor Park

Cranbourne Dr
Magna
Parva
Ranleigh Wk
Acacia Wk
Nairn Cl
Welbeck
Aran
Burnsall
Mons
Wensley Cl
Cm Pl
Swon Cl

I

End

West End Farm

Eastmoor Pk

Little La

Grange Ct Rd
Beech Cl

Lane

Ferrers Lane

2

Cross Lane

Ayres End La

Ayres End

12

Ayres End Lane

3

A1081

4

HARPENDEN ROAD

21 11

5

Cheapside Farm

Sandridgebury

15

16

CH**E**dwick Bury
F
G
H

Aley Green	53 E5	Church End	39 G5	Hart Hill	5 G1	Lower Sundon	22 C2	Stanbridge	2
Ansells End	57 H4	Church End	51 F5	Hatching Green	72 B1	Luton	4 E6	Stanbridgeford	2
Ayres End	75 H2	Church End	71 E3	Hexton	11 F5	Mackerye End	65 G5	Stopsley	5
Barton-le-Clay	10 B4	Cockernhoe Green	35 H4	Higham Gobion	11 E1	Mangrove Green	36 B4	Streatley	1
Batford	69 G1	Cold Harbour	65 E4	High Town	4 C2	Markyate	61 F4	Studham	5
Beecroft	20 A3	Darleyhall	47 E2	Hockliffe	18 D3	Marsh Farm	33 E1	Sundon Park	3
Bidwell	30 C2	Downside	41 G5	Holywell	59 E2	Moor End	48 C1	Tea Green	3
Biscot	44 A1	Dunstable	3 H5	Honeywick	38 C5	New Mill End	63 H1	Tebworth	1
Bower Heath	65 F3	East Hyde	64 B1	Houghton Regis	31 F5	New Town	54 B1	Tilsworth	2
Bramingham	23 G4	Eaton Bray	38 D5	Kensworth	51 G5	Parkside	31 E3	Tingrith	
Breachwood Green	47 G3	Eaton Green	38 A4	Kensworth Lynch	52 A5	Park Town	5 F7	Toddington	
Bury Park	43 H5	Edlesborough	48 B2	King's Walden	37 H5	Pegsdon	17 G1	Totternhoe	3
Caddington	53 F2	Fancott	20 D1	Kinsbourne Green	63 F4	Pepperstock	54 A5	Upper Sundon	2
Capability Green	54 C2	Farley Hill	43 H5	Leagrave	32 C4	Peters Green	57 E5	Wandon End	4
Chalgrave	20 B2	Flamstead	66 A2	Leasey Bridge	69 H5	Redbourn	71 F1	West Hyde	6
Chalton	21 F4	Friar's Wash	66 A1	Lea Valley	69 H1	Redbournbury	72 A5	Westoning	
Chaul End	42 D4	Great Offley	27 F3	Lewsey Farm	31 H5	Roe End	60 B5	Whipsnade	5
Cheverell's Green	60 D5	The Green	58 B1	Ley Green	37 H3	Round Green	44 C1	Wingfield	2
Childwick Green	72 D5	Harlington	13 H1	Lilley	25 H3	Sewell	39 H1	Winsdon Hill	
Chiltern Green	56 C3	Harpenden	68 B4	Limbury	33 F3	Sharpenhoe	8 D5	Wood End	6
Church End	18 B2	Harpenden Common	68 D5	Lower End	38 C2	Slip End	54 A4	Woodside	5

USING THE STREET INDEX

Street names are listed alphabetically. Each street name is followed by its postal town or area locality, the Postcode District, the page number, and the reference to the square in which the name is found.

Standard index entries are shown as follows:

Abbey Dr *LTNE* LU2 ....5 G1

Street names and selected addresses not shown on the map due to scale restrictions are shown in the index with an asterisk:

Abbotswood Pde *LTNE* LU2 * 5 G1

GENERAL ABBREVIATIONS

ACC.	ACCESS	CTYD	COURTYARD	HLS	HILLS	MWY	MOTORWAY	SE	SOUTH E
ALY	ALLEY	CUTT	CUTTINGS	HO	HOUSE	N	NORTH	SER	SERVICE A
AP	APPROACH	CV	COVE	HOL	HOLLOW	NE	NORTH EAST	SH	SH
AR	ARCADE	CYN	CANYON	HOSP	HOSPITAL	NW	NORTH WEST	SHOP	SHOPPI
ASS	ASSOCIATION	DEPT	DEPARTMENT	HRB	HARBOUR	O/P	OVERPASS	SKWY	SKY
AV	AVENUE	DL	DALE	HTH	HEATH	OFF	OFFICE	SMT	SUM
BCH	BEACH	DM	DAM	HTS	HEIGHTS	ORCH	ORCHARD	SOC	SOC
BLDS	BUILDINGS	DR	DRIVE	HVN	HAVEN	OV	OVAL	SP	S
BND	BEND	DRO	DROVE	HWY	HIGHWAY	P	PALACE	SPR	SPR
BNK	BANK	DRY	DRIVEWAY	IMP	IMPERIAL	PAS	PASSAGE	SQ	SQ
BR	BRIDGE	DWGS	DWELLINGS	IN	INLET	PAV	PAVILION	ST	STR
BRK	BROOK	E	EAST	IND EST	INDUSTRIAL ESTATE	PDE	PARADE	STN	STA
BTM	BOTTOM	EMB	EMBANKMENT	INF	INFIRMARY	PH	PUBLIC HOUSE	STR	STRE
BUS	BUSINESS	EMBY	EMBASSY	INFO	INFORMATION	PK	PARK	STRD	STRA
BVD	BOULEVARD	ESP	ESPLANADE	INT	INTERCHANGE	PKWY	PARKWAY	SW	SOUTH W
BY	BYPASS	EST	ESTATE	IS	ISLAND	PL	PLACE	TDG	TRAC
CATH	CATHEDRAL	EX	EXCHANGE	JCT	JUNCTION	PLN	PLAIN	TER	TERR
CEM	CEMETERY	EXPY	EXPRESSWAY	JTY	JETTY	PLNS	PLAINS	THWY	THROUGHW
CEN	CENTRE	EXT	EXTENSION	KG	KING	PLZ	PLAZA	TNL	TUN
CFT	CROFT	F/O	FLYOVER	KNL	KNOLL	POL	POLICE STATION	TOLL	TOLLW
CH	CHURCH	FC	FOOTBALL CLUB	L	LAKE	PR	PRINCE	TPK	TURNPI
CHA	CHASE	FK	FORK	LA	LANE	PREC	PRECINCT	TR	TR
CHYD	CHURCHYARD	FLD	FIELD	LDG	LODGE	PREP	PREPARATORY	TRL	TR
CIR	CIRCLE	FLDS	FIELDS	LGT	LIGHT	PRIM	PRIMARY	TWR	TO
CIRC	CIRCUS	FLS	FALLS	LK	LOCK	PROM	PROMENADE	U/P	UNDERPA
CL	CLOSE	FLS	FLATS	LKS	LAKES	PRS	PRINCESS	UNI	UNIVERS
CLFS	CLIFFS	FM	FARM	LNDG	LANDING	PRT	PORT	UPR	UPP
CMP	CAMP	FT	FORT	LTL	LITTLE	PT	POINT	V	V
CNR	CORNER	FWY	FREEWAY	LWR	LOWER	PTH	PATH	VA	VAL
CO	COUNTY	FY	FERRY	MAG	MAGISTRATE	PZ	PIAZZA	VIAD	VIAD
COLL	COLLEGE	GA	GATE	MAN	MANSIONS	QD	QUADRANT	VIL	V
COM	COMMON	GAL	GALLERY	MD	MEAD	QU	QUEEN	VIS	VI
COMM	COMMISSION	GDN	GARDEN	MDW	MEADOWS	QY	QUAY	VLG	VILL
CON	CONVENT	GDNS	GARDENS	MEM	MEMORIAL	R	RIVER	VLS	VIL
COT	COTTAGE	GLD	GLADE	MKT	MARKET	RBT	ROUNDABOUT	VW	V
COTS	COTTAGES	GLN	GLEN	MKTS	MARKETS	RD	ROAD	W	W
CP	CAPE	GN	GREEN	ML	MALL	RDG	RIDGE	WD	WO
CPS	COPSE	GND	GROUND	ML	MILL	REP	REPUBLIC	WHF	WHA
CR	CREEK	GRA	GRANGE	MNR	MANOR	RES	RESERVOIR	WK	W
CREM	CREMATORIUM	GRG	GARAGE	MS	MEWS	RFC	RUGBY FOOTBALL CLUB	WKS	WA
CRS	CRESCENT	GT	GREAT	MSN	MISSION	RI	RISE	WLS	W
CSWY	CAUSEWAY	GTWY	GATEWAY	MT	MOUNT	RP	RAMP	WY	WY
CT	COURT	GV	GROVE	MTN	MOUNTAIN	RW	ROW	YD	YA
CTRL	CENTRAL	HGR	HIGHER	MTS	MOUNTAINS	S	SOUTH	YHA	YOUTH HOS
CTS	COURTS	HL	HILL	MUS	MUSEUM	SCH	SCHOOL		

POSTCODE TOWNS AND AREA ABBREVIATIONS

AMP/FLIT/BLC	Ampthill/Flitwick/Barton-le-Clay	DUN/WHIP	Dunstable/Whipsnade	LTN	Luton	RMKS/WB	Rural Milton Keynes south/Woburn
BERK	Berkhamsted	HARP	Harpenden	LTNE	Luton east	STALE/WH	St Albans east/Wheathampstead
DUN/HR/TOD	Dunstable/Houghton Regis/Toddington	HTCH/STOT	Hitchin/Stotfold	LTNN/LIM	Luton north/Limbury		
		HTCHE/RSTV	Hitchin east/Rural Stevenage	LTNW/LEA	Luton west/Leagrave	STALW/RED	St Albans west/Redbourn
		LBUZ	Leighton Buzzard				

A

Abbey Dr *LTNE* LU2	5 G1
Abbey Ms *DUN/WHIP* LU6	41 E5
Abbey Wk *LTN* LU1	4 E5
Abbots Wood Pde *LTNE* LU2 *	5 G1
Abbots Wood Rd *LTNE* LU2	5 G1
Abercorn Rd *LTNW/LEA* LU4	31 H5
Abigail Cl *LTNN/LIM* LU3	33 G4
Abingdon Rd *LTNW/LEA* LU4	32 C5
Acacia Wk *HARP* AL5	73 F1
Acorn Cl *LTNE* LU2	34 D5
Acworth Crs *LTNW/LEA* LU4	32 C3
Addington Wy *LTNW/LEA* LU4	32 C5
Adelaide St *LTN* LU1	4 A5
Adstone Rd *LTN* LU1	53 F3
Aidans Cl *DUN/WHIP* LU6	40 A2
Ailsworth Rd *LTNN/LIM* LU3	33 G2
Airport Approach Rd *LTNE* LU2	45 H3
Airport Wy *LTN* LU1	54 C3
Albemarle Cl *LTNW/LEA* LU4	31 H5
Albert Ct *DUN/WHIP* LU6	3 F6
Albert Rd *LTN* LU1	54 C1
Albert St *STALW/RED* AL3	61 E4
Albion Ct *LTNE* LU2	4 C2
Albion Rd *LTNE* LU2	4 C3
Albion St *DUN/WHIP* LU6	2 C4
Albury Cl *LTNN/LIM* LU3	23 G4
Aldbanks *DUN/WHIP* LU6	40 B2
Aldenham Cl *LTNW/LEA* LU4	31 H5
Alder Crs *LTNN/LIM* LU3	33 G5
Alders End La *HARP* AL5	68 B2
Alderton Cl *LTNE* LU2	35 G5
Aldhous Cl *LTNN/LIM* LU3	33 H5
Aldwickbury Crs *HARP* AL5	69 F3
Aldwick Rd *HARP* AL5	69 G4
Alesia Rd *LTNN/LIM* LU3	33 E2
Alexandra Av *LTNN/LIM* LU3	33 H5
Alfred St *DUN/HR/TOD* LU5	3 F4
Alfriston Cl *LTNE* LU2	35 G5
Allenby Av *DUN/HR/TOD* LU5	42 A2
Allen Cl *DUN/HR/TOD* LU5	3 G5
Allendale *LTNN/LIM* LU3	23 G5
All Saints Rd *DUN/HR/TOD* LU5	30 D3
Alma Farm Rd *DUN/HR/TOD* LU5	12 A4
Alma Link *LTN* LU1	4 B4
Alma St *LTN* LU1	4 B4
Alpine Wy *LTNN/LIM* LU3	22 D5
Alsop Cl *DUN/HR/TOD* LU5	30 D2
Althorp Rd *LTNN/LIM* LU4	44 A2
Alton Rd *LTN* LU1	54 D1
Attwood *HARP* AL5	69 F5
Alwyn Cl *LTNE* LU2	44 C1
Alzey Gdns *HARP* AL5	69 F4
Amberley Cl *HARP* AL5	68 D2
LTNE LU2	35 H4
Ambleside *HARP* AL5	69 F2
LTNN/LIM LU3	33 F3
Ambrose La *HARP* AL5	64 B5
Amenbury La *HARP* AL5	68 C3
Ames Cl *LTNN/LIM* LU3	23 F4
Amhurst Rd *LTNW/LEA* LU4	43 E4
Andover Cl *LTNW/LEA* LU4	32 C2
Angel Cl *LTNW/LEA* LU4	32 D5
Angels La *DUN/HR/TOD* LU5	30 D3
Angus Cl *LTNW/LEA* LU4	32 A5
Anmer Gdns *LTNW/LEA* LU4	32 B2
Annabies La *HARP* AL5	62 D5
Anstee Rd *LTNN/LIM* LU4	32 B2
Anthony Gdns *LTN* LU1	54 B1
Aplins Cl *HARP* AL5	68 B2
Apollo Cl *DUN/HR/TOD* LU5	3 H6
Appleby Gdns *DUN/WHIP* LU6	2 C7
Applecroft Rd *LTNE* LU2	35
Apple Glebe *AMP/FLIT/BLC* MK45	10
Applewood Cl *HARP* AL5	68
Aran Cl *HARP* AL5	73
Arbour Cl *LTNN/LIM* LU3	24
Arbroath Rd *LTNN/LIM* LU3	24
The Arcade *LTNW/LEA* LU4	44
Archway Pde *LTNN/LIM* LU3 *	33
Archway Rd *LTNW/LEA* LU4	33
Arden Gv *HARP* AL5	73
Arden Pl *LTNE* LU2	44
Ardleigh Gn *LTNE* LU2	44
Ardley Ct *DUN/WHIP* LU6	5
Arenson Wy *DUN/HR/TOD* LU5	4
Argyll Av *LTNN/LIM* LU3	44
Armitage Gdns *LTNW/LEA* LU4	44
Arnald Wy *DUN/HR/TOD* LU5	3
Arncliffe Crs *LTNE* LU2	34

Nd Cl AMP/FLIT/BLC MK45......10 A5
TNE LU2 ....35 E5
on St LTN LU1 ....33 E2
el CI LTNW/LEA LU4 ....4 C7
del Rd LTNN/LEA LU4 ....43 C1
y Dr AMP/FLIT/BLC MK45......10 A4
urnham Rd LTN LU1 ....43 H4
roft DUN/WHIP LU6 ....40 B2
roft DUN/HR/TOD LU5 ....69 G4
roft Rd LTNE LU2 ....5 F5
ale Gdns LTNN/LIM LU3 ....23 G4
Dr HTCHE/RSTV SG4 * 65 H1
ield Wy LTNN/LIM LU3 ....5 C5
Gv DUN/HR/TOD LU5 ....3 C5
y Gdns HARP AL5 ....3 H4
al LTNN/LEA LU4 ....43 H3
on Rd DUN/WHIP LU6 ....2 A1
N LU1 ....54 C1
on Sq LTNN/LIM LU3 ....30 D2
ree Rd LTN LU1 ....30 D2
y Av LTNN/LEA LU4 ....22 C5
well Pk HARP AL5 ....69 F1
well Wk HARP AL5 ....68 C3
y Cl LTNN/LIM LU3 ....9 E1
y Gn LTNE LU2 ....45 H1
y Rd LTNN/LEA LU4 ....44 D5
rstone Rd LTNW/LEA LU4.......22 D5
all Cl LTNN/LIM LU3 ....22 D5
rey Gdns LTNE LU2 *.............32 B2
rey La STALW/RED AL3..........45 E2
rey Pl LTNE LU2 * 45 E2
ustus Rd LBUZ LU7 ....18 C3
ustus Wk LBUZ LU7 * 18 C3
on Rd LTNN/LIM LU3 ....33 H2
bury Av LTNE LU2 ....34 B4
nue Grimaldi
Avenue DUN/WHIP LU6..........33 G5
Av LTNN/LEA LU4 ....40 A4
indale Rd LTN LU1 ....44 A3
CI LTNN/LIM LU3 ....33 H2
scombe Cl DUN/WHIP LU6 ......40 B5
res End La HARP AL5 ....75 F5
garth Cl HARP AL5 ....43 E2
garth Rd STALW/RED AL3 ....71 E1

B

k St LTNE LU2 ....4 D2
gers Ga DUN/WHIP LU6 ....40 A3
ingham Rd HARP AL5 ....68 A4
wicks Cl LTNN/LIM LU3 ....33 E1
y St LTN LU1 ....4 E7
ers La DUN/WHIP LU6 ....59 G1
er St LTN LU1 ....54 C1
ewell Cl LTNW/LEA LU4 ....42 C2
combe Cl LTNE LU2 ....35 G4
lock Cl LTNN/LIM LU3 ....31 H5
our Ct HARP AL5 ....2 E1
more Wd LTNN/LIM LU3 ....23 H4
ville Wd HARP AL5 * 73 E2
nytton Rd LTNW/LEA LU4 ....33 H4
rk Cl LTNW/LEA LU4 ....32 C4
kside Cl DUN/HR/TOD LU5 ......30 C5
ford Rd LTNE LU2 ....45 H2
king Cl LTNW/LEA LU4 ....32 A3
ley Brow DUN/WHIP LU6 ....30 A5
e Barleycorn LTNN/LIM LU3 * ..4 A2
leyfield Wy
ingdale DUN/WHIP LU6 ....30 C3
ley Ri HARP AL5 * 32 C5
leyvale LTNN/LIM LU3 ....55 E5
lings Rd HARP AL5 ....72 D2
nard Rd LTN LU1 ....43 A5
nfield Av LTNE LU2 ....34 B3
nfield Ct HARP AL5 ....69 E4
nfield Rd HARP AL5 ....69 E4
ns Dene HARP AL5 ....32 C2
nston Cl LTNE LU2 ....45 H2
ntie Av DUN/WHIP LU6 ....39 E3
rons Rw HARP AL5 ....69 F5
rowby Cl LTNE LU2 ....45 H2
ton Av DUN/HR/TOD LU5 ....3 H5
ton Rd AMP/FLIT/BLC MK45.....9 F5
ton Rd
HTCH/STOT SG5 ....34 A1
LTNE LU2 ....23 H2
ssett Cl STALW/RED AL3.........71 F2
ford Mi HARP AL5 * 69 F2
ford Rd HARP AL5 ....64 A4
h Rd LTNN/LIM LU3 ....44 B1
e Baulk LTNE LU2 ....25 H5
y Cl LTNW/LEA LU4 ....32 B2
lam Dell LTNE LU2 ....40 A4
con Av DUN/WHIP LU6 ....40 A4
consfield LTNE LU2 ....5 J5
con Wy LBUZ LU7 ....28 B5
dtlove Rd LTNW/LEA LU4 ....31 H4
le St DUN/WHIP LU6 ....2 A2
nley Cl LTNE LU2 ....46 A1
umont Hall La
umont Rd LTNN/LIM LU3 ....43 F5
ckburry Cl LTNE LU2 ....46 A1
ckham Cl LTNE LU2 ....34 B1
cks Cl STALW/RED AL3 ....60 D4
ford Gdns LTNE LU2 ....4 B2
ford Rd
AMP/FLIT/BLC MK45...............10 A2
DUN/HR/TOD LU5 ....30 C2
LTN LU1 ....4 B5
ch Cl DUN/WHIP LU6 ....51 G1
HARP AL5 ....73 E2
chfield Cl
STALW/RED AL3 * 71 F2

Beech Gn DUN/WHIP LU6 ....40 B2
Beech Hl LTN LU1 ....35 G1
Beeching Cl HARP AL5 ....54 D5
Beech Rdg HARP AL5 ....63 F4
Beech St DUN/WHIP LU6 ....51 G2
LTN LU1 ....44 A3
Beech Tree Wy
DUN/HR/TOD LU5 ....30 D3
Beechwood Ct DUN/WHIP LU6 ..40 B4
Beechwood Rd LTNW/LEA LU4 ..33 E4
Beecroft Wy DUN/WHIP LU6 .....40 B5
Beesonend La STALW/RED AL3 ..71 H5
The Belfry LTNE LU2 ....34 C2
Belgrave Rd LTNW/LEA LU4 .....32 D5
Bell Cl AMP/FLIT/BLC MK45 ......2 C5
Bellerby Ri LTNW/LEA LU4 ....32 B2
Belmont Rd LTN LU1 ....44 A4
Belper Rd LTNW/LEA LU4 ....43 E1
Belsize Rd LTNW/LEA LU4 ....31 C5
Belvedere Rd LTNN/LIM LU3 .....33 H3
Bembridge Gdns LTNN/LIM LU3 ..43 H2
Ben Austins STALW/RED AL3 * ..71 E3
Benington Cl LTNE LU2 ....34 D3
Bennetts Cl DUN/WHIP LU6 ......2 C6
Benning Av DUN/WHIP LU6 ......40 B3
Benson Cl LTNN/LIM LU3 ....53 F1
Beresford Rd LTNW/LEA LU4 .....45 G2
Berkeley Pth LTNE LU2 ....2 E3
Bernard Cl DUN/WHIP LU6 ....2 E5
Berrow Cl LTNE LU2 ....46 A1
Berry Leys LTNN/LIM LU3 ....33 E1
Besford Cl LTNE LU2 ....45 H1
Bethune Cl LTN LU1 ....44 D5
Betjeman Cl HARP AL5 * 69 E5
Bettespol Mdw STALW/RED AL3 ..71 E1
Beverley Rd LTNW/LEA LU4 .....43 F2
Bewdley Cl HARP AL5 ....73 F1
Bexhill Rd LTN LU1 ....44 A1
Bibshall Crs DUN/WHIP LU6 .....41 E5
Bideford Gdns LTNN/LIM LU3 ...34 B4
Bidwell Hi DUN/HR/TOD LU5 ....30 C3
Bigthan Rd DUN/WHIP LU6 ......43 H5
Bilton Wy LTN LU1 ....43 F5
Binder Cl LTNW/LEA LU4 ....31 G4
Binder Ct LTNW/LEA LU4 * 31 G4
Binham Cl LTNE LU2 ....34 B1
Birchen Gv LTNE LU2 ....34 D5
Birch Link LTNW/LEA LU4 ....44 A2
Birch's Cl LBUZ LU7 ....18 D5
Birch Side DUN/WHIP LU6 ....44 B1
Birch Wy HARP AL5 ....69 E4
Birdsfoot La LTNN/LIM LU3 .....33 H2
Birling Dr LTNE LU2 ....35 G3
Birtley Cft LTNE LU2 ....46 A2
Biscot Rd LTNN/LIM LU3 ....44 A1
Bishopscote Rd LTNN/LIM LU3 ..33 H5
Blackburn Rd
DUN/HR/TOD LU5 ....30 D5
Blackhill LBUZ LU7 ....28 D2
Blackhorse La STALW/RED AL3 ..71 E1
Blacksmiths Rw
STALW/RED AL3 * 61 E4
Black Swan La LTNN/LIM LU3 ..33 G3
Blackthorn Dr LTNE LU2 ....35 G4
Black Thorn Rd
DUN/HR/TOD LU5 ....31 E2
Blakelands
AMP/FLIT/BLC MK45................10 B5
Blakeney Dr LTNW/LEA LU4 .....34 A1
Blandford Av LTNE LU2 ....34 B2
Blaydon Rd LTNE LU2 ....34 C3
Blenheim Crs LTNN/LIM LU3 ....44 A1
Bloomfield Av LTNE LU2 ....45 E2
Bloomfield Rd HARP AL5 ....68 B1
Bloomsbury Gdns
DUN/HR/TOD LU5 ....31 F3
Blows Rd DUN/HR/TOD LU5 .....41 E5
Bluebell Wood Cl LTN LU1 ....43 F4
Blundell Rd LTNW/LEA LU4 ......33 G5
Blyth Pl LTN LU1 ....4 B7
Bodmin Rd LTNW/LEA LU4 ......33 F4
Bolingbroke Rd LTN LU1 ....43 A5
Bolney Gn LTNE LU2 ....34 E5
Bolton Rd LTN LU1 ....44 A5
Bonnick Cl LTN LU1 ....44 A5
Booth Pl DUN/WHIP LU6 ....38 C5
Borough Rd DUN/WHIP LU6 .....2 A6
Borrowdale Av DUN/WHIP LU6 ..41 E5
Boscombe Rd
DUN/HR/TOD LU5 ....41 E1
Bosmore Rd LTNN/LIM LU3 ......33 F3
Bottom Dr DUN/WHIP LU6 ......49 H1
Bowbrook V LTNE LU2 ....46 A1
Bower Ct DUN/WHIP LU6 ....48 D1
Bower Heath La HARP AL5 ....65 E6
Bower La DUN/WHIP LU6 ....48 D1
Bower's Pde HARP AL5 ....68 C3
Bowers Wy HARP AL5 ....68 C2
Bowland Crs DUN/WHIP LU6 ....40 C5
Bowling Cl HARP AL5 ....68 A1
Bowling Green La LTNE LU2 .....3 F7
Bowmans Cl DUN/WHIP LU6 .....3 F7
Bowmans Wy DUN/WHIP LU6 ...3 F7
Boxgrove Cl LTNE LU2 ....35 G3
Boxted Cl LTNW/LEA LU4 ....32 C5
Boyle Cl LTNE LU2 ....5 J3
Braceby Cl LTNN/LIM LU3 ....33 F2
Brache Cl STALW/RED AL3 ....71 E2
Brackendale Gv HARP AL5 ....67 H1
LTNN/LIM LU3 ....53 G3
Bracklesham Gdns LTNE LU2 ....35 H5
Bradford Cl LTNW/LEA LU4 ......31 H5
Bradford Rd DUN/HR/TOD LU5 ..20 C5
Bradford Wy
DUN/HR/TOD LU5 ....20 B1
Bradgers Hill Rd LTNE LU2 ....34 C4
Bradley Rd LTNW/LEA LU4 ....42 D2
Bradshaws Cl
AMP/FLIT/BLC MK45................10 A4
Braintree Cl LTNW/LEA LU4 .....68 B1
Bramble Cl HARP AL5 ....68 B1
LTNW/LEA LU4 ....32 C4
Bramble Rd DUN/WHIP LU6 .....32 C4
Bramhanger Acre
LTNN/LIM LU3 ....32 D1

Bramingham Rd
LTNN/LIM LU3 ....33 F2
Brampton Cl HARP AL5 ....69 F3
Brampton Ri HARP AL5 ....41 E5
Brandreth Av DUN/WHIP LU6 ...5 K2
Branton Cl LTNE LU2 ....46 A1
Brantwood Rd LTN LU1 ....44 A5
Brays Rd LTNE LU2 ....35 F5
Brazier Cl AMP/FLIT/BLC MK45 ..9 H4
Breadcroft La HARP AL5 ....68 D2
Brecon Cl LTN LU1 ....4 A7
Brendon Av LTNE LU2 ....45 G2
Brentwood Cl
LTNN/LIM LU3 ....54 A1
Bretts Md LTN LU1 ....54 A1
Brewers Hill Rd DUN/WHIP LU6 ..40 B2
Brian Rd DUN/HR/TOD LU5 ......8 A5
Briar Cl LTNE LU2 ....35 G4
Brickly Rd LTNN/LIM LU3 ....32 B3
Bridgeman Dr
DUN/HR/TOD LU5 ....31 F3
Bridge St LTN LU1 ....4 C4
Brierley Cl DUN/WHIP LU6 ....59 H4
LTNE LU2 ....45 H1
Brightwell Av DUN/WHIP LU6 ...45 H1
Brill Cl LTNE LU2 ....45 H1
Brimfield Cl LTNE LU2 ....45 H1
Bristol Rd LTNN/LIM LU3 ....33 G4
Britain St DUN/HR/TOD LU5 .....3 F5
Britannia Av LTNN/LIM LU3 .....33 H3
Brive Rd DUN/HR/TOD LU5 ......54 B2
Broadacres LTNE LU2 ....45 H1
Broadfields HARP AL5 ....68 B2
Broad Md LTNN/LIM LU3 ....33 C5
Broadstone Rd HARP AL5 ....75 E1
Broadwalk DUN/HR/TOD LU5 ....2 D4
Bromley Gdns
DUN/HR/TOD LU5 ....31 F3
Brompton Cl LTNN/LEA LU4 .....23 C5
Brompton Gdns LTNN/LIM LU3 ..23 C5
Brook Cl DUN/WHIP LU6 ....2 B4
Brooke End STALW/RED AL3 .....71 E3
Brookend Dr
AMP/FLIT/BLC MK45................9 H5
Brookfield Av
DUN/HR/TOD LU5 ....31 E4
Brookfield Pk
DUN/WHIP LU6 * 39 E3
Brooklands Cl LTNW/LEA LU4 ...32 C2
Brookside HARP AL5 ....48 D2
LTNN/LIM LU3 ....23 C5
Broom Cnr HARP AL5 ....69 E4
Brooms Rd LTNE LU2 ....5 F2
Broughton Av
LTNE LU2 ....12 A4
HARP AL5 ....34 A3
Browning Rd HARP AL5 ....69 E2
LTNW/LEA LU4 ....42 A1
Brownlow Av DUN/WHIP LU6 ...48 D5
Brownlow Ri DUN/WHIP LU6 ....39 E3
Brown's Cl LTNW/LEA LU4 ....32 D5
Brown's Crs DUN/HR/TOD LU5 ..7 H4
Broxley Md LTNW/LEA LU4 ......32 C5
Brunel Cl LTNW/LEA LU4 ....31 C5
Brunel Rd LTNW/LEA LU4 ....31 G5
Brunswick St LTNE LU2 ....4 D2
Brussels Wy LTNN/LIM LU3 ......22 D4
Bryant Cl HARP AL5 ....68 C1
Bryant Wy DUN/HR/TOD LU5 ...12 B5
Bryony Wy DUN/WHIP LU6 .....40 A2
Buchanan Dr LTNE LU2 ....5 K2
Buckingham Dr LTNE LU2 ....45 H1
Buckle Cl LTNN/LIM LU3 ....33 F1
Buckwood Av DUN/HR/TOD LU5 ..3 C5
Buckwood La DUN/WHIP LU6 ...59 E2
Buckwood Rd DUN/WHIP LU6 ...60 A3
Bull Pond La DUN/WHIP LU6 ....2 D6
Bull Rd HARP AL5 ....68 D4
The Bungalows HARP AL5 ....69 E1
Bunhill Cl DUN/WHIP LU6 ....40 B5
Bunting Rd LTNW/LEA LU4 ......32 C3
Bunyan Rd AMP/FLIT/BLC MK45 ..7 G2
Bunyans Cl LTNN/LIM LU3 ....33 G5
Bunyans Wk DUN/HR/TOD LU5 ..7 H5
Burford Cl LTNW/LEA LU4 ....23 F4
Burges Cl LTNN/LIM LU3 ....51 F1
Burnham Rd LTNE LU2 ....45 H2
Burnsall Pl HARP AL5 ....73 E1
Burnt Cl LTNN/LIM LU3 ....33 F1
Burr Cl AMP/FLIT/BLC MK45 ....10 A3
Burr's Pl LTN LU1 ....4 D6
Burr St DUN/HR/TOD LU5 ....8 A5
LTNE LU2 ....4 D2
Bury Cl DUN/HR/TOD LU5 ......13 H1
Bury La LTNN/LIM LU3 ....15 G5
Bury Park Rd LTN LU1 ....44 A3
Bury Ri LBUZ LU7 ....28 D3
Burywick HARP AL5 ....72 D2
Bush Cl DUN/HR/TOD LU5 ....12 B4
Bushmead Rd LTNE LU2 ....34 C3
Butely Rd LTNW/LEA LU4 ....32 B3
Bute St LTN LU1 ....4 D4
Butlin Rd LTN LU1 ....43 H4
Buttercup Cl DUN/WHIP LU6 ....12 B4
Butterfield Green Rd LTNE LU2 ..35 E2
Buttermere Av DUN/WHIP LU6 ..41 E5
Butterworth Pth LTNE LU2 ....4 A5
Buxton Rd LTN LU1 ....4 C5
Buzzard Rd LTNW/LEA LU4 ......32 A3
Byfield Cl DUN/WHIP LU6 ....41 E5
LTNW/LEA LU4 ....41 B2
Byron Rd HARP AL5 ....68 C2
Byslips Rd DUN/WHIP LU6 ....59 F4

C

Caddington Common
STALW/RED AL3 ....61 E1
Caddington Pk LTN LU1 * 42 B2
Cades Cl LTN LU1 ....43 G5
Cadcutt Cl DUN/HR/TOD LU5 ...43 G5
Caleb Cl LTNW/LEA LU4 ....43 H1
Calverton Rd LTNN/LIM LU3 .....33 F2
Calnwood Rd LTNN/LIM LU3 .....33 F2
Camberley Pl HARP AL5 ....73 F1
Cambridge St LTN LU1 ....4 E1
Camford Wy LTNW/LEA LU4 .....22 A5
Camomile Gv LTNN/LIM LU3 ....23 G5
Camp Dr DUN/HR/TOD LU5 .....30 D5
Campian Cl DUN/WHIP LU6 ......40 A2
Campion Rd
AMP/FLIT/BLC MK45................7 H2
Canberra Gdns LTNN/LIM LU3 ..22 C5
Candale Cl DUN/WHIP LU6 ....41 E5
Cannon La LTNE LU2 ....33 F4
Canterbury Cl LTNW/LEA LU4 ...33 F4
Cantilupe Cl DUN/WHIP LU6 ....38 B5
Capron Rd DUN/HR/TOD LU5 ...2 B4
LTNW/LEA LU4 ....33 E4
Cardiff Gv LTN LU1 ....4 A4
Cardiff Rd LTN LU1 ....4 A4
Cardigan Ms LTN LU1 * 4 A4
Cardigan St LTN LU1 ....4 A4
Carfax Cl LTNW/LEA LU4 ....43 E2
Carisbrooke Rd HARP AL5 ....43 E2
LTNW/LEA LU4 ....43 E2
Carlisle Cl DUN/WHIP LU6 ....40 D5
Carlton Bank HARP AL5 ....68 D3
Carlton Cl LTNN/LIM LU3 ....44 A1
Carlton Crs LTNN/LIM LU3 ....44 A1
Carlton Rd HARP AL5 ....68 C2
Carmelite Rd LTNN/LEA LU4 ....32 A5
Carnegie Gdns LTNN/LIM LU3 ...23 F5
Carol Cl LTNN/LIM LU3 ....33 H4
Carpenders Cl HARP AL5 ....63 H5
Carsdale Cl LTNN/LIM LU3 ....33 G2
Carteret Rd LTNE LU2 ....45 G2
Carterweys DUN/HR/TOD LU5 ..3 J1
Cartmel Dr DUN/WHIP LU6 ......40 C5
Castle Cl DUN/WHIP LU6 ....59 E3
Castle Croft Rd LTN LU1 ....43 G5
Castle Hill Rd DUN/WHIP LU6 ...38 D3
Castle Ri STALW/RED AL3 ....69 H2
Castle St LTN LU1 ....2 A6
Catchacre DUN/WHIP LU6 ....40 A2
Catesby Gn LTNN/LIM LU3 ....33 H2
Catherall Rd LTNN/LIM LU3 .....33 H2
Catsbrook Rd LTNN/LIM LU3 ....33 H2
Cavalier Cl LTNN/LIM LU3 ....33 G2
Cavan Rd STALW/RED AL3 ....71 E1
Cavendish Rd LTNN/LIM LU3 ....33 H2
STALW/RED AL3......................60 D3
Cedar Cl LTNW/LEA LU4 ....31 C5
The Cedars DUN/WHIP LU6 .....2 E6
HARP AL5 ....68 D3
Celandine Dr LTNN/LIM LU3 ....23 C5
Cemetery Rd
DUN/HR/TOD LU5 ....30 D4
Central Av DUN/WHIP LU6 ......58 A1
Chad La STALW/RED AL3 ....62 A4
Chadwell Cl LTNE LU2 ....44 D2
Chadwick Cl DUN/WHIP LU6 ....2 B3
Chalfont Wy LTNE LU2 ....45 F1
Chalgrave Rd LBUZ LU7 ....20 A2
Chalkdown LTNE LU2 ....34 D3
Chalk Hl LTNE LU2 ....36 B4
Challney Cl LTNW/LEA LU4 ......42 D1
Chalton Hts LTNW/LEA LU4 .....21 F4
Chalton Rd LTNW/LEA LU4 ......32 C3
Chamberlaines HARP AL5 ....63 E4
Chandos Rd LTNW/LEA LU4 .....43 F2
Chapel Cl DUN/WHIP LU6 ....12 B4
Chapel Rd HTCHE/RSTV SG4 ....47 G2
Chapel St LTN LU1 ....4 C5
Chapel Viad LTN LU1 ....4 C5
Chapter House Rd
LTNW/LEA LU4 ....42 A1
Chard Dr LTNN/LIM LU3 ....23 H4
Charles St LTNE LU2 ....4 E1
Charlwood Rd LTNW/LEA LU4 ...42 B2
Charmbury Ri LTNE LU2 ....35 E4
Charndon Cl LTNN/LIM LU3 ......34 C5
Chartwell Dr LTNE LU2 ....34 C5
Chase St LTN LU1 ....54 C1
Chatsworth Rd LTNW/LEA LU4 ..43 H2
Chatteris Cl LTNE LU2 ....32 D4
Chatton Cl LTNE LU2 ....46 A1
Chaucer Rd LTNW/LEA LU4 .....43 E2
Chaul End La LTN LU1 ....42 C3
Chaul End Rd LTN LU1 ....42 C3
Chaworths Gn LTNW/LEA LU4 ..33 H5
Cheapside LTN LU1 ....4 C4
Cheapside Sq LTN LU1 * 4 C4
Chelsea Gdns
LTNW/LEA LU4 ....31 F3
Chelsworth Cl LTNE LU2 ....35 H5
Cheney Cl DUN/HR/TOD LU5 ....12 B4
Cheney Rd LTNW/LEA LU4 ....32 C3
The Chennies HARP AL5 ....69 E5
Chequer Cl LTN LU1 * 4 A3
Chequer Rd STALW/RED AL3 ....71 F3
Chequers Hi STALW/RED AL3 ...66 A2
The Chequers HARP AL5 ....48 D1
Chequer St LTN LU1 ....4 D6
Cherry Tree Cl LTNE LU2 ....45 E2
Chertsey Cl LTNE LU2 ....45 G3
Chesford Rd LTNE LU2 ....35 G5
Cheslyn Cl LTNE LU2 ....46 A1
Chester Av LTNW/LEA LU4 ......33 E5
Chester Cl LTNW/LEA LU4 ....33 E5
Chesterton Av HARP AL5 ....69 E5
Chestnut Av LTNN/LIM LU3 .....22 B4
Chestnut Cl AMP/FLIT/BLC MK45 ..9 H5
The Chevenalds DUN/WHIP LU6 ..41 E5
Cheverells Cl STALW/RED AL3 ...60 D4
Cheviot Rd LTNN/LIM LU3 ....33 F2
Cheyne Rd LTNN/LIM LU3 ....30 B5
Chichester Cl DUN/HR/TOD LU5 ..3 H6
Chiltern Av DUN/WHIP LU6 ......3 G1
Chiltern Gdns LTNW/LEA LU4 ..33 E5
Chiltern Pk DUN/HR/TOD LU5 ...3 G1
Chiltern Ri LTNN/LIM LU3 ....4 A7

Chiltern Rd
AMP/FLIT/BLC MK45................10 A4
DUN/WHIP LU6 ....2 A5
The Chilterns DUN/WHIP LU6 ...59 H1
Chobham St LTN LU1 ....4 E6
Chobham Wk LTN LU1 ....4 D6
The Chowns HARP AL5 ....72 C2
Christian Cl DUN/HR/TOD LU5 ..13 G1
Church Cl DUN/HR/TOD LU5 .....2 E4
DUN/WHIP LU6 ....58 D5
Church Cft DUN/WHIP LU6 ....48 C3
Church End DUN/HR/TOD LU5 ...3 G3
STALW/RED AL3......................60 D5
STALW/RED AL3......................71 E3
Churchfield HARP AL5 ....69 E4
Churchfield Rd
DUN/HR/TOD LU5 ....30 D3
Church Ga DUN/WHIP LU6 ....48 C3
Church Gn DUN/WHIP LU6 ......39 F4
HARP AL5 ....68 C3
Church Green Rw HARP AL5 * ...68 C3
Churchill Cl LTNN/LIM LU3 ....15 F5
Churchill Rd
AMP/FLIT/BLC MK45................10 A4
DUN/WHIP LU6 ....51 F1
LBUZ LU7 ....18 B2
Church Md DUN/WHIP LU6 ......58 D5
Church Rd AMP/FLIT/BLC MK45 ..7 F1
AMP/FLIT/BLC MK45................10 A5
DUN/HR/TOD LU5 ....7 H5
DUN/WHIP LU6 ....59 F5
DUN/WHIP LU6 ....58 D5
HTCHE/RSTV SG4 ....59 F5
LTN LU1 ....54 A4
LTNN/LIM LU3 ....15 G4
LTNN/LIM LU3 ....22 B2
RMKS/WB MK17 ....6 B2
Church Sq DUN/HR/TOD LU5 ...12 B4
Church St DUN/HR/TOD LU5 ....2 E4
LTN LU1 ....4 E3
LTNE LU2 ....4 E5
Church Wk DUN/HR/TOD LU5 ...23 C5
Cicero Dr LTNN/LIM LU3 ....43 H2
Claremont Rd LTNW/LEA LU4 ...43 H2
Clarence Rd HARP AL5 ....68 B2
Clarendon Rd HARP AL5 ....68 D1
LTNE LU2 ....27 E3
Clarion Cl HTCH/STOT SG5 ......27 E3
Clarkes Pightle
AMP/FLIT/BLC MK45................10 A5
Clarkes Wy DUN/HR/TOD LU5 ..31 E4
Claverley Gn LTNE LU2 ....46 A1
Claydon Cl LTNN/LIM LU3 ....34 A1
Claydown Wy LTNN/LIM LU3 ...53 H5
Claygate Av HARP AL5 ....68 A2
Clay Hall Rd DUN/WHIP LU6 ....59 H2
The Cleavers DUN/HR/TOD LU5 ..12 B5
The Cleave HARP AL5 ....68 D3
Clevedon Rd LTNE LU2 ....45 F1
Cleveland Rd STALW/RED AL3 ..61 E4
Clifford Crs LTNW/LEA LU4 ......32 C3
Clifton Rd DUN/WHIP LU6 ....2 B3
LTN LU1 ....44 C4
Clinton Av LTNE LU2 ....34 D4
Cloisters HARP AL5 * 73 E1
Cloisters Rd LTNW/LEA LU4 .....32 B3
The Cloisters
DUN/HR/TOD LU5 * 3 F5
The Close HARP AL5 ....63 H5
LTNE LU2 ....34 D4
STALW/RED AL3......................61 E4
Clover Cl LTNW/LEA LU4 ....31 H5
Clydesdale Rd LTNW/LEA LU4 ..32 A5
The Coach House
AMP/FLIT/BLC MK45................10 A4
Cobden St LTNE LU2 ....4 D1
Coldharbour La HARP AL5 ....64 D5
Colebrook Av LTNN/LIM LU3 ....32 C1
Colemans Rd HTCHE/RSTV SG4 ..47 F2
Coleswood Rd HARP AL5 ....69 E5
Colin Rd LTNE LU2 ....44 D1
Collens Rd HARP AL5 ....72 D2
Collingdon St LTN LU1 ....4 A3
Collingtree LTNE LU2 ....35 F4
Collins Wd LTN LU1 * 53 E2
Coltsfoot Gn LTNW/LEA LU4 ....32 A3
Colwell Ri LTNE LU2 ....46 A1
Common La HARP AL5 ....22 A1
LTNN/LIM LU3 ....22 A1
Common Rd DUN/WHIP LU6 ....51 F5
The Common HARP AL5 ....63 F5
Comp Ga DUN/WHIP LU6 ....38 C5
The Comp DUN/WHIP LU6 ....38 D6
Compton Av LTNW/LEA LU4 ....32 D4
Concorde St LTNE LU2 ....4 E2
Conger La DUN/HR/TOD LU5 ...12 C4
Coniston Rd LTNN/LIM LU3 ......33 F3
Connaught Rd HARP AL5 ....68 D2
LTNW/LEA LU4 ....43 F2
Conquest Rd
DUN/HR/TOD LU5 ....31 F4
Constable Cl DUN/HR/TOD LU5 ..31 F3
Conway Cl LTNW/LEA LU4 ....32 C3
Conway Rd LTNW/LEA LU4 ......43 H2
Cookfield Cl DUN/WHIP LU6 .....40 A3
Cook's Meadow
DUN/WHIP LU6 ....48 C2
Coombe Dr DUN/WHIP LU6 .....40 A4
Coopers Meadow
STALW/RED AL3......................71 E1
Coopers Wy DUN/HR/TOD LU5 ..30 C4
Cooters End La HARP AL5 ....64 B5
Copenhagen Cl LTNE LU2 ....22 D5
Copper Beeches LTNW/LEA LU4 ..32 B4
Copperfields LTNW/LEA LU4 ....32 B4
Copperfields Cl
DUN/HR/TOD LU5 ....31 F4
The Coppins STALW/RED AL3 ...60 D4
Copse Wy LTNN/LIM LU3 ....22 D5
Copthorne LTNE LU2 ....35 H5
Coral Cl DUN/WHIP LU6 ....58 C5
Corbridge Dr LTNE LU2 ....46 A1

Corinium Gdns LTNN/LIM LU5 .....23 G5
Corncastle Rd LTN LU1 ....44 A3
Corncrake Cl LTNE LU2 ....35 G5
Cornei Cl LTN LU1 ....4 D5
Cornwall Rd HARP AL5 ....60 D4
Cornwall Rd HARP AL5 ....68 D2
Cosgrove Wy LTN LU1 ....4 D5
Cotefield LTNW/LEA LU4 ....32 C5
Cotswold Business Pk LTN LU1 .....32 C1
Cotswold Gdns LTNN/LIM LU3......32 C1
Court Dr DUN/HR/TOD LU5 ....2 D3
Courtfields HARP AL5 ....69 F3
Covent Garden Cl
   LTNW/LEA LU4 ....33 F5
Coverdale LTNW/LEA LU4 ....32 B2
Cowdray Cl LTN LU1 ....35 G5
Cow La DUN/WHIP LU6 ....48 C2
Cowper Ct STALW/RED AL3 ....60 D4
Cowper Rd STALW/RED AL3 ....60 D4
Cowper Rd HARP AL5 ....68 D5
   STALW/RED AL3 ....60 D4
Cowper St LTN LU1 ....54 C1
Cowridge Crs LTNE LU2 ....35 F5
Coyney Gn LTNN/LIM LU3 ....44 A2
Crabtree La HARP AL5 ....69 F1
Crabtree Wy DUN/HR/TOD LU5 .....2 D2
Cradock Rd LTNW/LEA LU4 ....42 B2
Cranbourne Rd HARP AL5 ....73 E1
Cranbrook Dr LTNN/LIM LU3 ....22 D5
Cranleigh Gdns LTNN/LIM LU3.....36 A5
Cravells Rd HARP AL5 ....73 E1
Crawley Cl LTN LU1 ....54 A5
Crawley Green Rd LTNE LU2 ....35 J4
Crawley Rd LTNN/LIM LU3 ....4 A2
Crecy Gdns STALW/RED AL3 ....71 E1
Crescent Rd LTNE LU2 ....4 E5
Crescent Rd LTNE LU2 ....4 E5
The Crescent
   DUN/HR/TOD LU5 ....12 B5
   LTNE LU2 ....53 E2
Cresta Cl DUN/HR/TOD LU5 ....42 A1
The Crest DUN/HR/TOD LU5 ....3 J3
   LTNN/LIM LU3 ....33 H1
Croft Cl HARP AL5 * ....
Croft Gn DUN/WHIP LU6 ....60 D5
Croft Rd LTNE LU2 ....35 F5
The Croft LTNN/LIM LU3 ....22 D5
Croftwell HARP AL5 ....69 H4
Cromer Wy LTNE LU2 ....53 H1
Cromwell Wk II LTNE LU2 ....4 B1
Cromwell Rd
   AMP/FLIT/BLC MK45 ....10 A5
   LTNN/LIM LU3 ....4 A1
Crosby Cl DUN/WHIP LU6 ....41 E5
   LTNN/LIM LU3 ....4 A1
Crosslands LTN LU1 ....53 E5
Cross La HARP AL5 ....73 E2
Crosspaths HARP AL5 ....63 G5
Cross St LTNE LU2 ....4 E1
Cross St North DUN/WHIP LU6 ....2 A2
Cross Wy HARP AL5 ....69 E1
Crossways DUN/HR/TOD LU5 ....31 E5
The Cross Wy LTN LU1 ....54 A1
Crouch Hall Gdns
   STALW/RED AL3 ....71 E1
Crouch Hall La STALW/RED AL3 ...71 E1
Crowland Rd LTNE LU2 ....35 G3
Crown St STALW/RED AL3 ....71 F2
Croxton Cl LTNN/LIM LU5 ....33 G1
Cubbington Cl LTNN/LIM LU3 ....53 G1
Cuffley Cl LTNN/LIM LU3 ....53 F5
Culverhouse Cl LTNN/LIM LU3 ......34 A4
Culworth Cl LTN LU1 ....53 E3
Cumberland Dr
   STALW/RED AL3 ....71 F2
Cumberland St
   DUN/HR/TOD LU5 ....30 D4
   LTN LU1 ....4 D6
Cumbria Cl DUN/HR/TOD LU5 .....31 G3
Curlew Rd LTNE LU2 ....53 H1
Curzon Rd LTNE LU2 ....44 A2
Cussen Pl LTNN/LIM LU3 * 32 D1
Cusworth Wy DUN/WHIP LU6 ......40 A2
Cutenhoe Rd LTN LU1 ....54 D1
Cutlers Gn LTNE LU2 ....46 B1
Cut Throat Av DUN/WHIP LU6 ......58 A2

D

Dagnall Rd DUN/WHIP LU6 ....49 G4
Dahlia Cl LTNE LU2 ....35 F5
Daiby Cl LTNW/LEA LU4................32 B4
Dale Cl DUN/HR/TOD LU5 ....12 B5
Dale Rd DUN/HR/TOD LU5 ....41 H2
   LTN LU1 ....44 A4
Dalewood HARP AL5 ....69 F5
Dalkeith Rd HARP AL5 ....69 E2
Dailing Dr DUN/HR/TOD LU5 ....31 E3
Dallow Rd LTN LU1 ....43 E3
Dalton Cl LTNN/LIM LU3 ....54 B5
Dammersey Cl STALW/RED AL3 ...60 F5
Dane Cl HARP AL5 ....65 E5
Dane Rd AMP/FLIT/BLC MK45 .....10 A5
   LTNN/LIM LU3 ....43 H1
Danvers Dr LTNN/LIM LU3 ....24 A4
Dark La HARP AL5 ....73 E1
Darley Rd LTNE LU2 ....46 D2
Daubeney Cl DUN/HR/TOD LU5....7 H3
Dawlish Rd LTNE LU2 ....45 E1
Deep Denes LTNE LU2 ....45 E1
The Deerings HARP AL5 ....72 C5
Delco Wy DUN/WHIP LU6 ....40 A3
Delfield Gdns LTN LU1 ....53 E2
Dell Cl HARP AL5 ....65 D1
Dellcot Cl LTNE LU2 ....35 F3
Dellcroft Wy HARP AL5 ....72 C1
Dell Rd DUN/HR/TOD LU5 ....30 D3
The Dell LTN LU1 ....53 E3
   LTNE LU2 ....53 E3
Delmerend La STALW/RED AL3 ...66 A3

Delphine Cl LTN LU1 ....43 G5
Denbigh Rd LTNN/LIM LU3 ....43 H1
Dencora Wy LTNN/LIM LU3 ....22 B5
Denham Cl LTNE LU2 ....23 E5
Denmark Cl LTNN/LIM LU3 ....23 E4
Denton Cl LTNW/LEA LU4 ....32 B4
Derby Rd LTNW/LEA LU4 ....42 C1
Derwent Av LTNN/LIM LU3 ....33 H1
Derwent Dr DUN/WHIP LU6 ....31 E1
Derwent Rd HARP AL5 ....63 G5
   LTNE LU2 ....5 G2
Devon Rd LTNE LU2 ....5 J2
Devonshire Rd HARP AL5 ....68 D2
Dewsbury Rd LTNW/LEA LU4 ....33 H2
Dexter Cl LTNN/LIM LU3 ....23 G5
Dickens La LBUZ LU7 ....29 E3
Dickinsons Fld HARP AL5 ....69 E5
Ditchling Cl LTNE LU2 ....35 G5
Ditton Gn LTNE LU2 ....45 H1
Dolmans Pl DUN/WHIP LU6 ....2 C5
Dolphin Dr DUN/HR/TOD LU5 ......31 F5
Dorchester Cl LTNN/LIM LU3 ....2 D3
Dordans Rd LTNW/LEA LU4 ....33 E4
Dorel Cl LTNW/LIM LU3 ....44 D1
Dorrington Cl LTNN/LIM LU3 ....44 A2
Dorset Ct LTN LU1 ....44 B5
Douglas Crs DUN/HR/TOD LU5 ....30 C5
Douglas Rd HARP AL5 ....68 B2
Dovedale LTNE LU2 ....34 C2
Dove House Cl DUN/WHIP LU6 ....48 D2
Dovehouse Hl LTNE LU2 ....45 H1
Dove House La DUN/WHIP LU6 ....59 E2
Dover Cl LTNN/LIM LU3 ....33 G5
Down Edge STALW/RED AL3 ....70 D2
Downlands LTNN/LIM LU3 ....32 C1
Downs Rd DUN/HR/TOD LU5 ....3 G5
   LTN LU1 ....44 A4
Downs Vw DUN/HR/TOD LU5 ......53 F1
Drapers Ms LTNN/LIM LU3 * 44 A2
Drayton Rd LTNW/LEA LU4 ....31 H5
The Drive HARP AL5 ....68 C3
Drovers Wy DUN/WHIP LU6 ....40 B3
Drury Cl DUN/HR/TOD LU5 ....31 E5
Drury La DUN/HR/TOD LU5 ....31 E5
Dudley St LTNE LU2 ....4 C2
Dukes Av LTNW/LEA LU4 ....58 A1
Duke St LTN LU1 ....4 D2
Dumfries St LTN LU1 ....4 B6
Duncombe Cl LTNN/LIM LU3 ....34 A2
Duncombe Dr
   DUN/HR/TOD LU5 ....41 G1
Dunraven Av LTN LU1 ....43 G5
Dunsby Rd LTNN/LIM LU3 ....33 G2
Dunsmore Rd LTN LU1 ....43 H5
Dunstable Cl LTNW/LEA LU4 ....43 G2
Dunstable Pl LTN LU1 ....4 B5
Dunstable Rd
   DUN/HR/TOD LU5 ....20 B3
   LTNE LU2 ....30 D4
   LTN LU1 ....49 E1
   DUN/WHIP LU6 ....58 D5
   LBUZ LU7 ....29 F2
   LTN LU1 ....52 A2
   STALW/RED AL3 ....66 D5
Dunstall Rd
   AMP/FLIT/BLC MK45 ....10 A5
Durbar Rd LTNW/LEA LU4 ....43 G2
Durham Rd LTNE LU2 ....5 H3
Durler Gdns LTN LU1 ....54 B1
Duxford Cl LTNN/LIM LU3 ....33 H1
Dyers Rd DUN/WHIP LU6 ....38 B4

E

Eagle Centre Wy
   LTNW/LEA LU4 ....32 B1
Eagle Cl LTNW/LEA LU4 ....32 A4
Earls Meade LTNE LU2 ....44 B2
Easedale Cl DUN/WHIP LU6 ....41 E5
Easingwold Gdns LTN LU1 ....43 F5
Eastcote Dr HARP AL5 ....73 F1
Eastcott Cl LTNE LU2 ....35 H2
East End DUN/HR/TOD LU5 ....31 E3
Eastern Av DUN/HR/TOD LU5 ....3 G3
Eastfield Cl LTNE LU2 ....35 G4
East Hl LTNE LU2 ....35 H2
Easthill Rd DUN/HR/TOD LU5 ....31 E3
Eastmoor Pk HARP AL5 ....73 H1
East St LTNE LU2 ....4 E5
Eaton Bray Rd DUN/WHIP LU6 .....38 C5
   DUN/WHIP LU6 ....48 A1
Eatongate Cl DUN/WHIP LU6 ....48 C2
Eaton Green Rd LTNE LU2 ....45 G3
Eaton Pk DUN/WHIP LU6 ....38 D5
Eaton Pl LTNE LU2 ....45 H2
Eaton Valley Rd LTNE LU2 ....5 K1
Ebenezer St LTN LU1 ....4 A3
Eddiwick Av DUN/HR/TOD LU5 ....31 F1
Edgcott Cl LTNN/LIM LU3 ....23 H4
Edgecote Cl LTN LU1 ....53 G5
Edgehill Gdns LTNN/LIM LU3 ....22 C5
Edgewood Dr LTNE LU2 ....35 G2
Edkins Cl LTNE LU2 ....34 C3
Edward St LTNW/LEA LU4 ....2 B3
   LTNE LU2 ....4 E1
Egdon Dr LTNE LU2 ....45 H2
Eighth Av LTNN/LIM LU3 ....32 D1
Elaine Gdns LTN LU1 ....33 G5
Elderberry Cl LTNE LU2 ....35 F4
Eldon Rd LTNW/LEA LU4 ....42 C1
Eleanor's Cross DUN/WHIP LU6 ....2 C4
Elgar Pth LTNE LU2 ....35 H5
Elizabeth St LTN LU1 ....4 B6
Elienhall Cl LTNN/LIM LU3 ....44 A2
Ellerdine La LTNN/LIM LU3 ....33 H4
Ellesmere Cl DUN/WHIP LU6 ....39 G5
Elliswick Rd HARP AL5 ....68 D2
Elm Av LTN LU1 ....33 G5
Elm Gv DUN/HR/TOD LU5 ....12 B4
Elmore Rd LTNE LU2 ....45 E2

Elm Park Cl DUN/HR/TOD LU5 .....31 F2
Elmside LTN/WHIP LU6 ....59 F1
Elmtree Av LTNE LU2 ....36 A5
Elmwood Crs LTNE LU2 ....34 C5
Elveden Cl LTNE LU2 ....34 C2
Elvington Gdns LTNN/LIM LU3 .....23 H4
Ely Wy LTNW/LEA LU4 ....32 D4
Emerald Rd LTNW/LEA LU4 ....33 H1
Emmer Gn LTNE LU2 ....45 E4
Empress Rd LTNN/LIM LU3 ....33 E4
Enderby Rd LTNN/LIM LU3 ....34 A1
Enfield Cl LTNN/HR/TOD LU5 ....31 F2
England Av DUN/WHIP LU6 ....30 A5
Englands La DUN/HR/TOD LU5 ......3 F4
Englehurst HARP AL5 ....69 E2
Ennerdale Av DUN/WHIP LU6 ....2 C7
Ennis Cl HARP AL5 ....73 F1
Ennismore Gn LTNE LU2 ....46 B2
Enslow Cl LTN LU1 ....53 E3
Enterprise Wy LTNN/LIM LU3 ....23 H5
Epping Wy LTNN/LIM LU3 ....23 G1
Ereswell Rd LTNN/LIM LU3 ....33 G4
Erin Cl LTNW/LEA LU4 ....43 G1
Escarpment Av
   DUN/WHIP LU6 ....58 A1
Eskdale LTNW/LEA LU4 ....32 C5
Essex Cl LTN LU1 ....5 J3
Evans Cl DUN/HR/TOD LU5 ....31 F4
Evedon Cl LTNN/LIM LU3 ....33 E4
Evelyn Rd DUN/HR/TOD LU5 ....41 H1
Evergreen Cl LTNN/LIM LU3 ....23 H1
Exton Av LTNE LU2 ....35 F1
Eyncourt Rd DUN/WHIP LU6 ....3 F1
Eynsford Cl LTNW/LEA LU4 ....32 D5

F

Fairfax Av LTNN/LIM LU3 ....32 D1
Fairfield Cl DUN/HR/TOD LU5 ....41 H2
   HARP AL5 ....69 F1
Fairfield Rd DUN/HR/TOD LU5 ....3 K2
Fairford Av LTNE LU2 ....34 C3
Fairgreen Rd LTN LU1 ....54 F3
Fairmead Av HARP AL5 ....69 E4
Fair Oak Dr LTNE LU2 ....34 D5
Fairway Cl HARP AL5 ....72 C2
Falcon Cl LTNW/LEA LU4 ....2 B2
Falconers Fld HARP AL5 ....67 H1
Falconers Rd LTNE LU2 ....5 K1
Faldo Rd AMP/FLIT/BLC MK45 ......9 G5
Fallowfield LTNN/LIM LU3 ....33 H4
Fallows Gn HARP AL5 ....68 A1
Falstone Gn LTNE LU2 ....46 A1
Faraday Cl LTNW/LEA LU4 ....32 C2
Faringdon Rd LTNW/LEA LU4 ....32 C5
Farley Farm Rd LTN LU1 ....53 H1
Farley Hl LTNE LU2 ....53 H2
Farm Av HARP AL5 ....68 B3
Farm Cl DUN/HR/TOD LU5 ....34 B1
Farm Cl LTN LU1 ....53 H2
Farm Gn LTN LU1 ....63 F2
Farm Rd DUN/HR/TOD LU5 ....34 B1
Farrer Top STALW/RED AL3 ....71 E4
Farrow Cl LTNN/LIM LU3 ....23 H4
Farr's La LTNE LU2 ....36 B5
Felbrigg Cl LTNE LU2 ....46 B1
Felix Av LTNE LU2 ....45 E1
Felmersham Ct LTN LU1 ....41 H4
Felmersham Rd LTN LU1 ....43 G4
Felstead Cl LTNE LU2 * 44 D1
Felstead Wy LTNE LU2 ....44 D1
Felton Cl LTNE LU2 ....45 H2
Fensome Dr DUN/HR/TOD LU5 ....31 E5
Fenwick Cl LTNN/LIM LU3 ....33 H3
Fenwick Rd DUN/HR/TOD LU5 .....45 G2
Ferndale Rd LTNE LU2 ....43 H4
Fernheath LTNN/LIM LU3 ....23 G4
Ferrars Cl LTNW/LEA LU4 ....42 B2
Ferrars La HARP AL5 ....73 H2
Field Cl HARP AL5 ....69 F5
Field End LTNW/LEA LU4 ....32 A3
Field Fare Gn LTNW/LEA LU4 ....32 A3
Fieldgate Rd LTNW/LEA LU4 ....32 D5
Filmer Rd LTNN/LIM LU3 ....33 E4
Finch Cl LTNW/LEA LU4 ....32 A4
Finley Rd HARP AL5 ....68 B3
Finsbury Rd LTNW/LEA LU4 ....32 D3
Finway LTN LU1 ....43 G3
Firbank Cl LTNN/LIM LU3 ....22 C5
First Av DUN/WHIP LU6 ....30 A5
The Firs HARP AL5 * 69 F2
Fisher Cl AMP/FLIT/BLC MK45 ......9 H4
Fish Farm St STALW/RED AL3 ......71 F2
Fish St STALW/RED AL3 ....71 F2
Fitzroy Av LTNN/LIM LU3 ....33 H5
Fitzwarin Cl LTNN/LIM LU3 ....33 E1
Five Oaks LTN LU1 ....3 J7
Five Springs LTNN/LIM LU3 ....33 E2
Flamsteadbury La
   STALW/RED AL3 ....61 E4
Flax Ms STALW/RED AL3 * 61 E4
Flint Cl LTNN/LIM LU3 ....33 E5
Flint Cottage STALW/RED AL3 ......71 F2
Flitwick Rd AMP/FLIT/BLC MK45...7 C1
Florence Av LTNN/LIM LU3 ....33 G5
Flowers Wy LTN LU1 ....4 C5
Flowton Gv HARP AL5 ....68 C5
Folly La LTN LU1 ....53 F2
Forge Cl LTNW/LEA LU4 ....21 C3
Forrest Crs LTNE LU2 ....35 E5
Foster Av DUN/HR/TOD LU5 ....30 D5
Foster Rd DUN/HR/TOD LU5 ....30 D5
Foston Cl LTNN/LIM LU3 ....33 H5
Fountains Rd LTNW/LEA LU4 ....34 A5
Fourth Av LTNN/LIM LU3 ....33 E1
Fovant Cl HARP AL5 ....73 E1
Foxbury Cl LTNE LU2 ....45 H1
Fox Dells DUN/WHIP LU6 ....51 E1
Foxhill LTNE LU2 ....34 C3
Francis St LTN LU1 ....44 A3
Frank Lester Wy LTNE LU2 ....45 H5

Franklin Av LTNN/LIM LU3 ....9 H4
Franklin Rd DUN/WHIP LU6 ....40 B5
Frederick St LTN LU1 ....4 C2
Frederick Street Pas LTNE LU2 ......4 C1
Freeman Av LTNW/LEA LU4 ....23 H5
Freemans Cl DUN/HR/TOD LU5 ....30 C4
Frenchmans Cl
   DUN/HR/TOD LU5 ....12 A5
French's Av DUN/WHIP LU6 ....40 A1
French's Ga DUN/WHIP LU6 ....40 A1
Freshwater Cl LTNN/LIM LU3 ....53 H1
Friars Cl LTN LU1 ....53 H1
Friars Wk DUN/HR/TOD LU5 ....34 D5
Friars Wy LTN LU1 ....53 H1
Friars Wash STALW/RED AL3 * 66 D2
Friary Fld DUN/WHIP LU6 ....17 D5
Friesian Cl LTNW/LEA LU4 ....32 A5
Friston Gn LTNE LU2 ....35 H2
Frome Cl LTNW/LEA LU4 ....33 E4
Front St LTN LU1 ....54 A5
Fulbourne Ct LTNW/LEA LU4 ....43 E1
Fulmore Cl HARP AL5 ....65 F5
Furlong La DUN/WHIP LU6 ....39 G4
Furness Av DUN/WHIP LU6 ....2 D7
Furrows LTNN/LIM LU3 ....33 H4
Furze Cl LTNE LU2 ....34 B1
Furzedown Ct HARP AL5 ....68 D4
Furzen Cl HARP AL5 ....51 E1

G

Gainsborough Dr
   DUN/HR/TOD LU5 ....31 F3
Gale Ct AMP/FLIT/BLC MK45 * 10 A5
Galliard Cl LTNN/LIM LU3 ....33 H4
Galston Rd LTNN/LIM LU3 ....22 D5
Garden Cl HARP AL5 ....72 C2
Gardenia Av LTNW/LEA LU4 ....33 G4
Garden Rd DUN/HR/TOD LU5 ....2 E7
Gardens End
   DUN/HR/TOD LU5 * 31 E5
Gardner's Cl DUN/WHIP LU6 ....40 A4
Garrett Cl DUN/WHIP LU6 ....51 F1
Garretts Mel LTNE LU2 ....55 H5
Gatehill Gdns LTNN/LIM LU3 ....33 H4
Gayland Av LTNE LU2 ....34 D5
Gayton Cl LTNN/LIM LU3 ....33 G4
Gelding Cl LTNW/LEA LU4 ....31 H3
Gilpin Gn HARP AL5 ....31 F5
Gilpin Gn HARP AL5 ....69 E5
Gilpin's Gn HARP AL5 ....69 E5
Gipsy La LTN LU1 ....2 B1
Gladstone Av LTN LU1 ....44 A4
Glaisdale LTNW/LEA LU4 ....32 C5
Glebe Gdns LTNN/LIM LU3 ....7 H4
Glemsford Cl LTNW/LEA LU4 ....32 B2
Glemsford Dr HARP AL5 ....68 A1
Gleneagles Gr LTNE LU2 ....34 C2
The Glen LTN LU1 ....53 E3
Globe Cl HARP AL5 ....69 E3
Gloucester Rd LTN LU1 ....4 E5
Gloucester Ter LTN LU1 * 4 B5
Godfreys Cl LTN LU1 ....43 H5
Gold Crest Rd LTNW/LEA LU4 ......32 A3
Goldstone Crs DUN/HR/TOD LU5...5 H5
Good Intent DUN/WHIP LU6 ....48 C2
Gooseberry Hl LTNN/LIM LU3 ......33 H1
Goose Gn LBUZ LU7 ....18 B3
Gordon St LTN LU1 ....4 A5
Gordons Wk HARP AL5 ....69 E4
Gorham Wy DUN/HR/TOD LU5 ....41 H1
Gorse Cnr HARP AL5 ....69 E4
Gorselands HARP AL5 ....68 D5
Goshawk Cl LTNW/LEA LU4 ....32 A4
Gosling Av HTCH/STOT SG5 ....27 E3
Goswell End Rd
   DUN/HR/TOD LU5 ....7 H4
Graham Gdns LTNN/LIM LU3 ....34 A4
Grampian Wy LTNN/LIM LU3 ....3 J7
Granary La HARP AL5 ....68 D5
Granby Av HARP AL5 ....69 E2
Granby Rd LTNW/LEA LU4 ....32 D5
Grange Av LTNW/LEA LU4 ....32 D4
Grange Court Rd HARP AL5 ....73 E1
Grange Farm Cl
   AMP/FLIT/BLC MK45 ....9 H4
Grange Gdns
   DUN/HR/TOD LU5 ....12 B5
Grange Rd AMP/FLIT/BLC MK45 ...9 H4
Gransden Cl LTNN/LIM LU3 ....33 G1
Grant Gdns HARP AL5 ....68 D2
Grantham Rd LTNW/LEA LU4 ....43 G2
Granville Rd LTN LU1 ....43 H3
Graphic Cl DUN/WHIP LU6 ....41 F5
Grasmere Av HARP AL5 ....69 E2
Grasmere Cl LTNN/LIM LU3 ....4 C7
Grasmere Rd LTNN/LIM LU3 ....33 H1
Grays Cl AMP/FLIT/BLC MK45 .....10 A4
Greatfield Cl HARP AL5 ....63 G5
Great Northern Rd
   DUN/WHIP LU6 ....3 F6
Green Acres LTNE LU2 ....25 H3
Greenacres Pk
   DUN/WHIP LU6 * 59 H1
Green Cl LBUZ LU7 ....28 B3
   LTNW/LEA LU4 ....32 B3

Greenfield Cl DUN/WHIP LU6 40
Greenfield Rd
   AMP/FLIT/BLC MK45 7
Greengate LTNN/LIM LU3 22
Greenhill Av LTNE LU2 34
Green La DUN/WHIP LU6 59
   LTNE LU2 35
   STALW/RED AL3 61
Green Lane Cl HARP AL5 69
Green Milverton LTNN/LIM LU3 33
Green Oaks LTNE LU2 53
Greenriggs LTNE LU2 * 46
Greenside Pk LTNE LU2 31
The Green DUN/HR/TOD LU5 31
   LTN LU1 48
   LTNE LU2 57
   STALW/RED AL3 63
Greenway HARP AL5 69
Greenways DUN/WHIP LU6 38
Gregories Cl LTNE LU2 45
Gregory Cl LTNE LU2 12
Greyfriars La HARP AL5 35
Grosvenor Rd LTNN/LIM LU3 33
Grove Av HARP AL5 55
Grovebury Cl DUN/WHIP LU6 41
Grove End LTN LU1 53
Grove Park Rd LTN LU1 53
Grove Rd DUN/HR/TOD LU5 31
   HARP AL5 69
   LTN LU1 4
   LTNE LU2 35
The Grove AMP/FLIT/BLC MK45 7
   LTN LU1 4
   LTNE LU2 55
Guernsey Cl LTNW/LEA LU4 31
Guildford St LTN LU1 4
Gurney Ct DUN/WHIP LU6 38

H

Haddon Rd LTNE LU2 5
Hadleigh Ct HARP AL5 73
Hadlow Down Cl
   LTNN/LIM LU3 34
Hadrian Av DUN/HR/TOD LU5 31
Hagdell Rd LTN LU1 54
Hailes Meadow HARP AL5 66
Half Moon La DUN/HR/TOD LU5 3
   LTN LU1 62
Half Moon Pl DUN/WHIP LU6 * 41
Halfway Av LTNW/LEA LU4 42
Halley's Wy DUN/HR/TOD LU5 31
Hailwicks Rd LTNE LU2 35
Halyard Cl LTNW/LEA LU4 32
Hambling Pl DUN/WHIP LU6 40
Hambro Cl LTNE LU2 64
Hammersmith Cl
   DUN/HR/TOD LU5 31
Hammersmith Gdns
   DUN/HR/TOD LU5 31
Hammond Ct LTN LU1 * 54
Hammond End La HARP AL5 72
Hammonds Hl HARP AL5 72
Hammondswick HARP AL5 72
Hampshire Wy LTNW/LEA LU4 31
Hampton Rd LTNW/LEA LU4 44
Hancock Dr LTNE LU2 34
Handcross Rd LTNE LU2 35
Hanover Pl
   AMP/FLIT/BLC MK45 10
Hanswick Cl LTNE LU2 45
Hanworth Cl LTNE LU2 34
Harbury Dell LTNN/LIM LU3 33
Harcourt St LTN LU1 54
Harding Cl LTNE LU2 53
Harding Pde HARP AL5 71
Hardwick Gn LTNN/LIM LU3 33
Harefield Rd LTN LU1 43
Harlestone Cl LTNN/LIM LU3 33
Harling Rd DUN/WHIP LU6 49
Harlington Rd
   DUN/HR/TOD LU5 8
   DUN/HR/TOD LU5 2
   LTNN/LIM LU3 22
Harold Rd AMP/FLIT/BLC MK45 ...10
Harpenden La STALW/RED AL3 71
Harpenden Ri HARP AL5 68
Harpenden Rd STALW/RED AL3 73
Harrington Hts
   DUN/HR/TOD LU5 * 30
Harris Ct AMP/FLIT/BLC MK45 10
Harris La HTCH/STOT SG5 27
Harrowden Rd LTNE LU2 45
Harry Scott Ct LTNW/LEA LU4 32
Hart Hill Dr LTNE LU2 5
Hart Hill La LTNE LU2 5
Hart La LTNE LU2 5
Hartley Rd LTNE LU2 5
Hartsfield Rd LTNE LU2 45
Hart Wk LTNE LU2 5
Hartwell Gdns HARP AL5 68
Harvest Ct LTNN/LEA LU4 32
Harvey Rd DUN/WHIP LU6 39
Harvey's Hl LTNE LU2 34
Hasketon Dr LTNW/LEA LU4 32
Haslingden Cl HARP AL5 68
Hastings Rd
   AMP/FLIT/BLC MK45 10
Hastings St LTN LU1 4
Hatching Green Cl HARP AL5 72
Hathaway Cl LTNW/LEA LU4 43
Hatters Wy LTN LU1 43
Havelock Ri LTNE LU2 44
Havelock Rd LTNE LU2 44
Haverdale LTNW/LEA LU4 32
Hawkfields LTNE LU2 44
Hawsley Rd HARP AL5 72
Hawthorn Av LTNE LU2 25

...thorn Cl DUN/WHIP LU6 ....2 E7
...orn Crs LTN LU1 ....69 F5
...croft LTNE LU2 ....34 C2
...La HARP AL5 ....53 E5
...hurst Rd LTNW/LEA LU4 ....42 C2
...La HARP AL5 ....55 F5
...ey Ct LTN/HR/TOD LU5 ....31 E5
...ng Dr LTNE LU2 ....35 G5
...market Rd LTNW/LEA LU4 ....31 C4
...on Cl LTN/HR/TOD LU5 ....23 H5
...bury Crs LTN LU1 ....44 A3
...lwood Cl LTNE LU2 ....4 A3
...ham Cl LTNW/LEA LU4 ....32 B4
...l Cl HARP AL5 ....68 D5
...field LTN LU1 ....43 H4
...field Rd LTN/LIM LU3 ....34 A4
...Heath HTCHE/RSTV SG4 ....47 F1
...on Dell LTNE LU2 ....46 A2
...en Cl LTNW/LEA LU4 ....32 B4
...edgerow LTNW/LEA LU4 ....31 C4
...y Ri LTNE LU2 ....12 A5
...nsley Cl LTNW/LEA LU4 ....32 B5
...wait Cl LTN LU1
...nett Rd LTNW/LEA LU4 ....33 E4
...ton Rd
...MP/FLIT/BLC MK45 ....10 B5
...La HARP AL5 ....25 F1
...wood Dr LTNE LU2 ....34 D5
...est St LTN LU1
...ing Cl LTNE LU2 ....45 H2
...ing Wy HARP AL5
...rs Rd STALW/RED AL3 ....61 E4
...am Rd
...MP/FLIT/BLC MK45 ....10 A3
...Banks LBUZ LU7 ....28 A3
...Beech Rd LTNN/LIM LU3 ....32 D1
...bury Rd LTNN/LIM LU3 ....44 A2
...Elms HARP AL5 ....72 C1
...field Av HARP AL5 ....69 E4
...field Dv HARP AL5 ....45 H1
...field Rd LTNW/LEA LU4 ....43 H2
...fields AMP/FLIT/BLC MK45 ....7 G1
...fields Cl DUN/HR/TOD LU5 ....42 A1
...a Firs Crs HARP AL5
...s Md LTNN/LIM LU3 ....33 C5
...hover Cl LTNE LU2 ....5 J1
...s Rdg HARP AL5 ....68 A1
...TNE LU2 ....45 G2
...st AMP/FLIT/BLC MK45 ....7 G1
...UN/HR/TOD LU5 ....12 B4
...UN/HR/TOD LU5 ....30 D4
...UN/WHIP LU6
...ARP AL5
...TCH/STOT SG5 ....27 E2
...st North DUN/WHIP LU6 ....2 C3
...st South DUN/WHIP LU6 ....2 E5
...n Town Rd
...a Vw STALW/RED AL3 ....61 E5
...n Wood Cl LTN LU1
...ary Cl LTN/HR/TOD LU5 ....32 D1
...ary Crs LTN LU1 ....44 A5
...orough Crs
...DUN/WHIP LU6 ....31 E1
...orough Rd LTN LU1 ....1 A7
...Cl HARP AL5 ....65 E5
...LBUZ LU7 ....19 H4
...TNN/LIM LU3 ....34 A1
...crest Av LTNE LU2 ....34 A1
...croft DUN/WHIP LU6 ....40 A2
...Croft Cl LTNW/LEA LU4 ....32 B2
...Milford HARP AL5 ....65 F5
...Pickford HARP AL5 ....32 C1
...Side DUN/HR/TOD LU5 ....30 D3
...side Rd DUN/HR/TOD LU5 ....3 H7
...HARP AL5 ....68 B1
...TNE LU2 ....4 A1
...erfield La HARP AL5 ....22 B1
...op STALW/RED AL3 ....70 D1
...op Wk HARP AL5 ....68 C2
...view Crs LTNE LU2 ....34 A1
...kley Ct LBUZ LU7 ....41 G5
...on Av DUN/WHIP LU6 ....40 D5
...ton Wk DUN/HR/TOD LU5 ....17 H1
...thin Rd HTCH/STOT SG5 ....17 H1
...TNE LU2 ....4 E2
...erfield La HARP AL5 ....68 C2
...kley Ct LBUZ LU7 ....18 C5
...kliffe Rd LBUZ LU7 ....19 F4
...kwell Ring LTNW/LEA LU4 ....32 B3
...croft Rd HARP AL5 ....69 F1
...ford Wy LTNN/LIM LU3 ....23 H4
...gate Dr LTNW/LEA LU4 ....32 A4
...kham Cl LTNW/LEA LU4 ....32 A4
...and Rd LTN/LIM LU3 ....43 H1
...ick's La DUN/WHIP LU6 ....51 F4
...ybush Hl LTNE LU2 ....26 B4
...ybush La HARP AL5 ....68 B1
...ybush Rd LTNE LU2 ....45 H1
...y Farm Cl LTN LU1
...y La HARP AL5 ....65 G2
...y St LTN LU1 ....4 C6
...y Wk HARP AL5 ....69 F3
...mbrook Av LTNN/LIM LU3 ....34 A3
...nfield Cl
...HR/TOD LU5 * 12 A5

..........54 B1
Holmscroft Rd LTNN/LIM LU3 ....33 F2
Holmwood Cl LTN/HR/TOD LU5 ....3 H1
Hoits Meadow STALW/RED AL3 ....71 F1
Holtsmere Cl LTNE LU2 ....45 H2
Holywell Cl DUN/WHIP LU6 ....58 D5
Holywell Rd DUN/WHIP LU6 ....58 D5
Home Cl LTNE LU2 ....32 C4
Home Ct LTNW/LEA LU4 * 32 C4
Homedale Dr LTNW/LEA LU4 ....42 D1
Home Farm Wy
AMP/FLIT/BLC MK45 ....7 G1
Homerton Rd LTNN/LIM LU3 ....33 G2
Homestead Wy LTN LU1 ....54 A1
Honeygate LTNE LU2 ....58 C4
Honeywick La DUN/WHIP LU6 ....58 C4
Honiton Ms LTN/LIM LU3 ....33 E2
Hoo St LTN LU1 * 54 C1
Hornsby Cl LTNE LU2 ....45 G2
Horsham Cl LTNE LU2 ....35 H5
Horsler Cl AMP/FLIT/BLC MK45 ....10 A5
Houghton Pde D LTNW/LEA LU4 * 40 C1
Houghton Park Rd
DUN/HR/TOD LU5 ....31 G2
Houghton Rd
DUN/HR/TOD LU5 ....50 C5
Howard Cl LTNN/LIM LU3 ....53 G4
Howard Pl DUN/WHIP LU6 ....5 G7
Howes La AMP/FLIT/BLC MK45 * 7 G1
How Fld HARP AL5 ....68 A1
Huckleberry Cl LTNN/LIM LU3 ....25 C5
Hucklesby Wy LTNE LU2 ....4 B2
Humberstone Cl
LTNW/LEA LU4 ....43 E1
Humberstone Rd
LTNW/LEA LU4 ....43 E1
Humphrey Talbot Av
DUN/WHIP LU6 ....58 B2
Humphrys Rd
DUN/HR/TOD LU5 ....31 F5
Hunston Cl LTNW/LEA LU4 ....32 B3
Hunts Cl LTN LU1 ....44 A5
Hurlock Cl DUN/WHIP LU6 ....40 C5
Hurlock Wy LTNW/LEA LU4 ....32 C5
Hurst Wy LTN/LIM LU3 ....33 E3
Hyde Cl HARP AL5 ....64 D5
Hyde La LTNE LU2 ....53 F2
Hyde View Rd HARP AL5 ....64 D5

I

Ickley Cl LTNW/LEA LU4 ....32 B3
Icknield Rd LTNW/LEA LU4 ....33 F4
Icknield St DUN/WHIP LU6 ....2 C3
Icknield Wy BERK HP4 ....58 A4
DUN/WHIP LU6 ....49 E5
DUN/WHIP LU6 ....49 H1
LTNN/LIM LU3 ....33 G2
Icknield Way Pth
AMP/FLIT/BLC MK45 ....15 G2
DUN/HR/TOD LU5 ....12 D3
DUN/WHIP LU6 ....29 H4
HTCH/STOT SG5 ....17 H4
LTNN/LIM LU3 ....14 D4
Ilford Cl LTNE LU2 ....35 G5
Imberfield LTNW/LEA LU4 ....32 C5
Index Dr DUN/WHIP LU6 ....3 G7
Ingram Gdns LTNE LU2 ....34 B2
Inkerman St LTN LU1 ....4 B4
Isle of Wight La
DUN/WHIP LU6 ....50 D3
Ivel Cl AMP/FLIT/BLC MK45 ....10 B4
Ivinghoe Wy DUN/WHIP LU6 ....2 C5
Ivory Cl DUN/WHIP LU6 ....40 A2
Ivy Rd LTN LU1

J

Jacksons Cl DUN/WHIP LU6 ....48 C2
James Ct LTN LU1 ....4 C7
Jameson Rd HARP AL5 ....68 D1
Jardine Wy DUN/HR/TOD LU5 ....3 J7
Jaywood LTNE LU2 ....35 G5
Jeans Wy DUN/HR/TOD LU5 ....3 K4
Jeremiah Cl
AMP/FLIT/BLC MK45 ....10 A4
Jersey Rd LTNW/LEA LU4 ....32 A5
Jillifer Rd LTNW/LEA LU4 ....32 A5
John Bunyan Trail
AMP/FLIT/BLC MK45 ....15 F2
HTCHE/STOT SG5 ....16 B1
LTNE LU2 ....25 G3
LTNN/LIM LU3 ....23 H3
John St LTN LU1 ....4 D5
Jubilee Cl DUN/WHIP LU6 ....2 B2
Jubilee St LTNE LU2 ....4 F2
Julius Cl LTNN/LIM LU3 ....33 F1
Juniper Cl LTNW/LEA LU4 ....43 E1

K

Katherine Dr
DUN/HR/TOD LU5 ....3 K1
Keaton Cl DUN/HR/TOD LU5 ....31 F3
Keeble Cl LTNE LU2 ....46 A2
Keepers Cl LTNE LU2 ....45 G1
Kelling Wy LTNE LU2 ....24 A5
Kelvin Cl LTN LU1 ....4 C7
Kempsey Cl LTNE LU2 ....46 A2
Kendal Cl LTNN/LIM LU3 ....32 D1
Kendale Rd LTNW/LEA LU4 ....42 B1
Kenilworth Rd LTN LU1 ....44 A3
Kennel La HARP AL5 ....63 E4
Kenneth Rd LTNE LU2 ....45 J2
Kennington Rd LTNN/LIM LU3 ....43 H1

Kensington Cl
DUN/HR/TOD LU5 ....31 G4
Kensworth Rd DUN/WHIP LU6 ....59 E5
Kent Cl AMP/FLIT/BLC MK45 ....7 G2
Kent Rd DUN/HR/TOD LU5 ....31 F4
LTN LU1 ....43 F3
Kershaw Cl LTNW/LEA LU4 ....23 G5
Kestrel Wy LTNW/LEA LU4 ....32 A5
Keswick Cl DUN/WHIP LU6 ....2 D7
Ketton Cl LTNE LU2 ....5 H5
Keymer Cl LTNE LU2 ....35 G5
Kidner Cl LTNE LU2 ....35 G5
Kilby Rd LBUZ LU7 ....18 D5
Kilmarnock Dr LTNE LU2 ....34 C5
Kimberley Cl LTNN/LIM LU3 ....31 G5
Kimberwell Cl
DUN/HR/TOD LU5 ....20 B1
Kimpton Bottom HARP AL5 ....70 C2
Kimpton Rd LTNE LU2 ....57 G4
LTNE LU2 ....5 H7
King Croft Rd HARP AL5 ....69 F5
Kinghamway LTNE LU2 ....4 C1
Kingsbury Av LTN/HR/TOD LU5 ....3 K3
Kingsbury Ct
DUN/WHIP LU6 * 2 E4
Kingsbury Gdns
DUN/HR/TOD LU5 ....41 H2
Kingscroft Av LTN/HR/TOD LU5 ....2 D3
Kingsdown Av LTNE LU2 ....34 B4
Kingsland Cl DUN/WHIP LU6 ....4 E7
Kingsland Ct LTN LU1 ....4 E7
Kingsley Rd LTNN/LIM LU3 ....33 G5
Kings Md DUN/WHIP LU6 ....48 C3
Kingston Rd LTNE LU2 ....44 D2
King St DUN/HR/TOD LU5 ....30 D4
DUN/WHIP LU6 ....3 F6
LTN LU1 ....4 C4
LTNE LU2 ....61 E4
King's Walden Rd
HTCH/STOT SG5 ....27 E3
Kings Wy LBUZ LU7 ....28 C3
Kingsway DUN/HR/TOD LU5 ....2 E3
LTN LU1 ....43 G3
King William Cl
AMP/FLIT/BLC MK45 ....10 B3
Kinmoor Cl LTNN/LIM LU3 ....22 D5
Kinross Crs LTNN/LIM LU3 ....22 D5
Kinsbourne Cl HARP AL5 ....63 G5
Kinsbourne Crs HARP AL5 ....65 H5
Kinsbourne Green La
HARP AL5 ....67 F1
The Kipling LTNN/LIM LU3 ....33 H2
Kipling Wy HARP AL5 ....68 D5
Kirby Dr LTNN/LIM LU3 ....23 F4
Kirby Rd DUN/WHIP LU6 ....2 B5
Kirkdale Rd HARP AL5 ....2 C5
Kirkstone Dr DUN/WHIP LU6 ....40 D5
Kirkwick Av HARP AL5 ....68 B5
Kirkwood Rd LTNW/LEA LU4 ....31 H5
Knights Cl LTNW/LEA LU4 ....48 C1
Knights Fld LTNE LU2 ....44 B2
Knoll Ri LTNE LU2 ....34 C5
Knolls Vw DUN/HR/TOD LU5 ....38 D2
DUN/WHIP LU6 * 40 B4
Knotts Cl DUN/WHIP LU6 ....51 E1
Knowle Dr HARP AL5 ....69 F5
Kynance Cl LTNE LU2 ....35 E5

L

Laburnum Cl LTNN/LIM LU3 ....34 A1
Laburnum Gv LTNN/LIM LU3 ....33 H1
Lachbury Cl LTN LU1 ....43 G5
Ladyhill LTNW/LEA LU4 ....32 B2
Lakefield Av DUN/HR/TOD LU5 ....12 B5
Laker Ct LTNE LU2 ....44 B2
Lalleford Rd LTNE LU2 ....45 G2
Lamb La STALW/RED AL3 ....71 F2
Lambourn Dr LTNE LU2 ....34 C2
Lambourn Gdns HARP AL5 ....68 B1
Lambs Cl LTNN/LIM LU3 ....41 H2
Lamers Rd LTNE LU2 ....45 F1
Lamorna Cl LTNN/LIM LU3 ....33 F2
Lampitts Cross
LTNN/LIM LU3 * 33 G3
Lancaster Av LTNE LU2 ....24 A5
Lancaster Cl
AMP/FLIT/BLC MK45 ....10 B5
Lancing Rd LTNE LU2 ....35 H5
Lancot Av DUN/WHIP LU6 ....40 A3
Lancotbury Cl DUN/WHIP LU6 ....39 G4
Lancot Dr DUN/WHIP LU6 ....40 A3
Landrace Rd LTNW/LEA LU4 ....31 C4
The Lane LBUZ LU7 ....19 E1
LTNW/LEA LU4 ....21 G4
Langdale Av HARP AL5 ....69 F2
Langdale Cl DUN/WHIP LU6 ....2 C7
Langdale Rd DUN/WHIP LU6 ....2 C7
Langford Dr LTNE LU2 ....35 E5
Langham Cl LTNE LU2 ....34 B1
Langley St LTN LU1 ....4 D5
Lansdowne Rd LTNN/LIM LU3 ....44 A2
Laporte Wy LTNW/LEA LU4 ....45 F2
Lapwing Rd LTNW/LEA LU4 ....32 A4
The Larches HARP AL5 ....4 B1
Larkspur Gdns LTNN/LIM LU3 ....43 F1
Latimer Rd LTN LU1 ....4 D7
Launton Cl LTNW/LEA LU4 ....23 H4
Lavender Cl LTNE LU2 ....45 F1
Lawford Cl LTN LU1 ....44 C5
Lawn Gdns LTN LU1 ....44 B5
Lawns Cl HTCH/STOT SG5 ....27 E5
Lawrence End Rd LTNE LU2 ....57 E3
Lawrence Wy DUN/WHIP LU6 ....40 B1
Laxton Cl LTNE LU2 ....46 A2
Layham Dr LTNE LU2 ....45 H2
Leafield Cl LTNN/LIM LU3 ....33 F4
Leafields DUN/HR/TOD LU5 ....31 E2
Leaf Rd DUN/HR/TOD LU5 ....30 D2
Leagrave High St
LTNN/LIM LU3 ....31 H5

Leagrave Rd LTNN/LIM LU3 ....33 G5
Leamington Rd LTNN/LIM LU3 ....33 G1
Lea Rd HARP AL5 ....68 D1
LTN LU1 ....4 E5
Leasey Bridge La
STALW AL4 ....69 H5
Leathwaite Cl LTNN/LIM LU3 ....33 F3
Lea Valley Wk LTNE LU2 ....55 G1
Lea Wk HARP AL5 ....55 F5
Ledwell Rd LTN LU1 ....55 F5
Leghorn Crs LTNN/LIM LU3 ....32 A5
Leicester Rd LTNW/LEA LU4 ....43 G2
Leigh Cl LTNN/LIM LU3 ....12 B4
Leighton Cl DUN/WHIP LU6 ....2 A5
Leighton Rd DUN/HR/TOD LU5 ....12 A5
DUN/WHIP LU6 ....40 B4
DUN/WHIP LU6 ....48 A2
Lennox Gn LTNE LU2 ....46 B1
Lesbury Cl LTNE LU2 ....46 A2
Lester Ms LTNE LU2 * 4 F2
Leston Ct DUN/WHIP LU6 ....51 F1
Letchworth Rd LTNN/LIM LU3 ....32 C5
Levendale LTNN/LIM LU3 ....32 C3
Lewsey Park Ct
LTNW/LEA LU4 * 32 A4
Leyburn Rd LTNN/LIM LU3 ....33 E5
Leycroft Wy HARP AL5 ....69 C5
Leygreen Cl LTNE LU2 ....53 H2
Leyhill Dr LTN LU1 ....53 H2
Leyton Gn HARP AL5 ....68 C5
Leyton Rd HARP AL5 ....68 C5
Library Rd LTN LU1 ....4 C6
Liddel Cl LTNN/LIM LU3 ....33 G5
Lidgate Cl LTNW/LEA LU4 ....32 B2
Lighthorne Ri LTNN/LIM LU3 ....32 C5
Lilac Av LTNN/LIM LU3 ....22 C4
Lilac Wy HARP AL5 ....73 F1
Lilley Bottom HTCHE/RSTV SG4 ....57 F4
LTNE LU2 ....26 A4
Lilley Bottom Rd
HTCHE/RSTV SG4 ....37 C5
Lilleyhoo La LTNE LU2 ....26 B5
Limbrick Rd HARP AL5 ....73 F1
Limburn Rd LTNE LU2 ....33 F4
Lime Av LTNW/LEA LU4 ....33 H1
Lime Cl AMP/FLIT/BLC MK45 ....10 A4
Limetree Av LTNE LU2 ....63 E2
Lime Tree LTNN/LIM LU3 ....22 C4
Limewalk DUN/HR/TOD LU5 ....3 G5
Limmers Cl LTNW/LEA LU4 ....32 D4
Linbridge Wy LTNE LU2 ....46 A1
Lincoln Cl LTNW/LEA LU4 ....41 G5
Lincoln Rd LTNW/LEA LU4 ....43 H2
Lincoln Wy DUN/HR/TOD LU5 ....8 A5
Linden Cl DUN/HR/TOD LU5 ....3 C5
Linden Ct HARP AL5 ....68 D4
Linden Rd DUN/HR/TOD LU5 ....3 C5
LTNW/LEA LU4 ....33 E4
STALW/RED AL3 ....71 E1
The Lindens DUN/HR/TOD LU5 ....30 D4
Lindley Cl HARP AL5 ....64 C5
Lindsey Rd LTNE LU2 ....45 H2
Links Wy LTNE LU2 ....24 B5
Linnet Cl LTNN/LIM LU3 ....33 F1
Linney Head DUN/WHIP LU6 * 58 D3
Linwood Rd HARP AL5 ....55 F5
Lippitts Hl LTNE LU2 ....34 C3
Liscombe Rd DUN/HR/TOD LU5 ....3 J5
Liston Cl LTNW/LEA LU4 ....32 B3
Little Berries LTNN/LIM LU3 ....33 E1
Little Church Rd LTNE LU2 ....33 F5
Littlefield Rd LTNE LU2 ....35 F5
Littlegreen La LTN LU1 ....55 E4
Little La HARP AL5 ....73 E1
Little Meadow LTN LU1 * 53 H3
Little Wood Cft LTNN/LIM LU3 ....33 E1
Liverpool Rd LTN LU1 ....4 B3
Locarno Av LTNW/LEA LU4 ....31 H5
Lockhart Cl DUN/WHIP LU6 ....41 F5
Lockington Crs
DUN/HR/TOD LU5 ....3 K1
Lodge Gdns HARP AL5 ....68 C2
Loftus Cl LTNW/LEA LU4 ....32 B3
Lollard Cl LTNW/LEA LU4 ....31 H5
London Rd DUN/HR/TOD LU5 ....3 G5
HARP AL5 ....63 E5
LTN LU1 ....54 C2
STALW/RED AL3 ....61 E4
Longbrooke DUN/HR/TOD LU5 ....31 F4
Long Buftlers HARP AL5 ....69 F5
Long Cl LTNE LU2 ....35 G5
Longcroft Av HARP AL5 ....68 D5
Longcroft Dr
AMP/FLIT/BLC MK45 ....9 H5
Long Croft Rd LTNW/LEA LU4 ....43 G4
Long Cutt STALW/RED AL3 ....71 E1
Longfield Dr LTNW/LEA LU4 ....42 B2
Longfield Rd HARP AL5 ....69 E5
Long Hedge LTNW/LEA LU4 ....3 G4
Long La DUN/HR/TOD LU5 ....6 C4
Long Md DUN/HR/TOD LU5 ....30 D2
Long Meadow LTNE LU2 * 2 B5
STALW/RED AL3 ....61 E4
Lonsdale Cl LTN LU1 ....44 A5
Lords Cl LBUZ LU7 ....28 C5
Lord's Hl DUN/HR/TOD LU5 ....20 B4
Lords Md DUN/HR/TOD LU5 ....30 D2
Lords Meadow
STALW/RED AL3 ....71 E2
Lords Ter DUN/HR/TOD LU5 * 38 C5
Loring Rd DUN/WHIP LU6 ....40 B3
Lorrimer Cl LTNE LU2 ....46 A2
Lothair Rd LTNE LU2 ....35 E4
Lovers' Wk DUN/HR/TOD LU5 ....3 F5
Lovett Wy DUN/WHIP LU6 ....41 F5
Lower Harpenden Rd LTNE LU2 ....55 J1
LTNE LU2 ....64 A1
Lower Luton Rd HARP AL5 ....65 E5
LTNE LU2 ....65 E5
Lower Rd HTCHE/RSTV SG4 ....47 H2
Lowry Dr DUN/HR/TOD LU5 ....31 F3
Lowther Rd DUN/WHIP LU6 ....41 E5
Lucas Gdns LTNE LU2 ....23 H5
Lucerne Wy LTNN/LIM LU3 ....34 A4

Ludlow Av LTNE LU2 ....54 C2
Ludun Cl DUN/HR/TOD LU5 ....3 J4
Lullington Cl LTNE LU2 ....35 G5
The Luton Dr LTN LU1 ....55 E1
Luton La STALW/RED AL3 ....67 E4
Luton Rd AMP/FLIT/BLC MK45 ....15 G4
AMP/FLIT/BLC MK45 ....15 H1
DUN/HR/TOD LU5 ....12 C5
DUN/HR/TOD LU5 ....12 C5
HARP AL5 ....64 A5
LTN LU1 ....53 F2
LTNE LU2 ....26 C5
LTNE LU2 ....36 A5
LTNW/LEA LU4 ....53 E3
STALW/RED AL3 ....61 E2
Luton White Hl LTNE LU2 ....26 C5
Luxembourg Cl LTNN/LIM LU3 ....22 D5
Lybury La STALW/RED AL3 ....66 C5
Lye Hl HTCHE/RSTV SG4 ....47 F4
Lygetun Dr LTNN/LIM LU3 ....45 F1
Lynch Hl DUN/WHIP LU6 ....60 A1
Lyndhurst Cl HARP AL5 ....69 E2
Lyndhurst Dr HARP AL5 ....69 E2
Lyne Cl LTN LU1 ....44 A4
Lyneham Rd LTNE LU2 ....45 G2
Lynsey Cl STALW/RED AL3 ....67 E5
Lynwood Av LTNE LU2 ....35 E5

M

Macaulay Rd LTNW/LEA LU4 ....42 A1
Magna Cl HARP AL5 ....73 F1
The Magpies LTNE LU2 ....34 B2
Maidenbower Av
DUN/WHIP LU6 ....40 B2
Maidenhall Rd LTNW/LEA LU4 ....43 G1
Maidon Ct HARP AL5 ....68 D2
Malham Cl LTNW/LEA LU4 ....33 F5
Mallard Gdns LTNN/LIM LU3 ....33 G5
The Mallow LTNN/LIM LU3 * 33 F5
The Mall DUN/HR/TOD LU5 ....2 E5
Malms Cl DUN/WHIP LU6 ....51 F5
Malthouse Gn LTNE LU2 ....46 B2
Malvern Rd HARP AL5 ....43 H4
Maizeard Rd LTNN/LIM LU3 ....44 A2
Manchester Pl DUN/WHIP LU6 ....2 C5
Manchester St LTN LU1 ....4 B4
Mancroft Rd LTN LU1 ....52 D3
Mander Cl DUN/HR/TOD LU5 ....12 B4
Mangrove Rd LTNE LU2 ....35 C5
Manland Av HARP AL5 ....69 E2
Manland Wy HARP AL5 ....69 E2
Manning Pl LTNE LU2 ....46 A1
Manor Av LBUZ LU7 ....18 C3
Manor Cl AMP/FLIT/BLC MK45 ....7 G2
DUN/HR/TOD LU5 ....7 H5
Manor Farm Cl
AMP/FLIT/BLC MK45 ....10 A4
LTNE LU2 ....32 C5
Manor Gdns
AMP/FLIT/BLC MK45 ....7 F1
Manor Pk DUN/HR/TOD LU5 ....30 D4
Manor Park Dr
AMP/FLIT/BLC MK45 ....7 F1
Manor Rd AMP/FLIT/BLC MK45 ....10 B5
DUN/HR/TOD LU5 ....12 B5
LTN LU1 ....4 E6
LTNE LU2 ....53 E3
LTNN/LIM LU3 ....22 B2
STALW/WH AL4 ....69 H2
Mansdale Rd STALW/RED AL3 ....71 F5
Mansfield Rd LTNW/LEA LU4 ....43 H2
Manston Dr LTNE LU2 ....34 B4
Manton Rd DUN/WHIP LU6 ....49 H1
Manx Cl LTNW/LEA LU4 ....43 G1
Maple Rd HARP AL5 ....68 B5
Maple Rd East LTN LU1 ....43 H5
Maple Rd West LTNW/LEA LU4 ....43 H5
Maple Wy DUN/HR/TOD LU5 ....31 G2
DUN/WHIP LU6 ....59 G1
Marbury Pl LTNN/LIM LU3 * 33 F4
Mardale Av DUN/WHIP LU6 ....41 E5
Marina Dr DUN/WHIP LU6 ....40 A3
Market Sq DUN/HR/TOD LU5 ....12 C4
LTN LU1 ....43 H5
Markfield Cl LTNW/LEA LU4 ....34 A2
Markham Crs
DUN/HR/TOD LU5 ....41 G1
Markham Rd LTNN/LIM LU3 ....24 A5
Markyate Rd LTN LU1 ....61 C1
Marlborough Pl
DUN/WHIP LU6 ....12 B4
Marlborough Rd LTNN/LIM LU3 ....44 A2
Marlin Ct LTNW/LEA LU4 ....31 G4
Marlin Rd LTNW/LEA LU4 ....31 C5
Marlow Av LTN LU1 ....43 G5
Marquis Cl HARP AL5 ....69 F2
Marquis La HARP AL5 ....69 F2
Marriott Rd LTNW/LEA LU4 ....33 H2
Marshall Rd LTNE LU2 ....45 G1
Marshalls Wy STALW/WH AL4 ....69 H2
Marsh Rd LTNW/LEA LU4 ....32 D5
Marscom Cv LTNW/LEA LU4 ....23 H5
Marston Gdns LTNE LU2 ....34 B4
The Martindales LTNE LU2 * 5 F4
Maryport Rd LTNW/LEA LU4 ....43 G1
Masefield Ct HARP AL5 ....64 D5
Masefield Rd HARP AL5 ....64 D5
Masters Cl LTN LU1 ....53 H1
Matlock Crs LTNW/LEA LU4 ....42 C2
Matthew St DUN/WHIP LU6 ....2 C4
Maulden Cl LTNE LU2 ....45 G2
Maundsey Cl DUN/HR/TOD LU5 ....51 E1
Mayer Wy DUN/HR/TOD LU5 ....30 C5
Mayfield Cl HARP AL5 ....68 A1
Mayfield Rd DUN/HR/TOD LU5 ....41 F5
DUN/WHIP LU6 ....41 F5
LTNE LU2 ....35 F4
Mayne Av LTNW/LEA LU4 ....32 C4
Maypole Yd DUN/WHIP LU6 * 2 C4
May St LTN LU1 ....4 D7

Meadhook Dr
  AMP/FLIT/BLC MK45 ....9 H4
Meadow La DUN/HR/TOD LU5....30 D3
Meadow Rd DUN/HR/TOD LU5 ...12 A5
Meadow Rd LTNE LU2 ....33 H4
The Meadows
  HTCHE/RSTV SG4 ....47 G2
Meadow Wk HARP AL5 *..........71 F2
Meadow Wk HARP AL5 ....69 E4
Meadow Wy HTCH/STOT SG5.....27 E2
  LTN/LIM LU3 ....33 C3
Meads Cl DUN/HR/TOD LU5 ......50 D3
The Meads DUN/WHIP LU6.........48 C1
  LTNN/LIM LU3 ....33 C5
Meadway DUN/WHIP LU6.............2 A7
  HARP AL5 ....69 C5
Medina Rd LTNW/LEA LU4 ....49 C2
Medley Cl DUN/WHIP LU6...........48 D1
Medlows HARP AL5 ....68 A2
Mees Cl LTNN/LIM LU3 ....25 F4
Meiford Cl LTNE LU2 ....45 H2
Melson St LTN LU1 ....4 D4
Memorial Rd LTNN/LIM LU3 ....33 H4
Mendip Wy LTNN/LIM LU3 ....22 C5
Mentmore Crs DUN/WHIP LU6 ....51 E1
Mersey Pl HARP AL5 ....68 D5
The Mews HARP AL5 *................68 D5
Meyrick Av LTN LU1 ....44 A5
Middleton Rd LTN LU1 ....44 A5
Midhurst Gdns LTNN/LIM LU3 ...34 A5
Midland Rd LTNE LU2 ....4 C3
Milburn Cl LTNN/LIM LU3 ....23 H4
Miletree Crs DUN/WHIP LU6 ....41 F5
Mill End AMP/FLIT/BLC MK45 *.....8 C4
Mill End Cl DUN/WHIP LU6 ....48 D2
Millers Lay DUN/HR/TOD LU5 .....41 H1
Millers Wy DUN/HR/TOD LU5 .....30 C4
Milfield La LTN LU1 ....52 C3
Milfield Ms LTN LU1 ....52 D4
Milfield Rd LTNN/LIM LU3 ....33 H5
Milfield Wy LTN LU1 ....52 D3
Milliners Wy LTNN/LIM LU3 ....44 A2
Mill La AMP/FLIT/BLC MK45 ....9 H4
  HTCH/STOT SG5 ....11 F4
Mill Rd DUN/HR/TOD LU5 ....50 C4
  LBUZ LU7 ....28 A1
Mill St LTN LU1 ....14 A4
Millway HTCHE/RSTV SG4 ....47 F1
Mill Yd LTN LU1 * 4 D4
Milton Rd HARP AL5 ....68 D4
  LTN LU1 ....44 A5
Milton Wy DUN/HR/TOD LU5 .....31 F4
Milverton Gn LTNN/LIM LU3 ......33 C1
Minorca Wy LTNW/LEA LU4 ....32 A5
Miss Joans Ride DUN/WHIP LU6 .58 A2
Mistletoe HI LTNE LU2 ....45 C3
Mixes Hill Rd LTNE LU2 ....34 D5
The Moakes LTNN/LIM LU3 ....33 H4
Moat La LTNN/LIM LU3 ....33 H4
Mobley Gn LTNE LU2 ....35 F5
Moira Cl LTNN/LIM LU3 ....32 C2
Molescroft HARP AL5 ....63 H5
Monks Cl STALW/RED AL3 ....71 F2
Monmouth Cl
  DUN/HR/TOD LU5 ....12 A4
Monmouth Rd
  DUN/HR/TOD LU5 ....73 H5
Mons Cl HARP AL5 ....68 A2
Montague Av LTNW/LEA LU4 ....2 C6
Monton Cl LTNN/LIM LU3 ....33 F2
Montrose Av LTNN/LIM LU3 ....34 A5
Moore Crs DUN/HR/TOD LU5 .....31 E4
Moor End DUN/WHIP LU6...........48 D1
Moor End Cl DUN/WHIP LU6 ....48 D2
Moor End Rd DUN/WHIP LU6 ......48 D2
Moorland Gdns LTNE LU2 ....4 B2
Moorland Rd HARP AL5 ....64 D5
Moor St LTN LU1 ....44 A3
Morcambe Cl LTNW/LEA LU4 ......32 B5
Morcom Rd DUN/HR/TOD LU5....41 G5
Moreton Av HARP AL5 ....68 B2
Moreton End La HARP AL5 ....68 B2
Moreton End La HARP AL5 ....68 B2
Moreton Pl HARP AL5 ....68 B1
Moreton Rd North LTNE LU2 ....35 E1
Moreton Rd South LTNE LU2 ....45 E1
Morgan Cl LTNW/LEA LU4 ....33 E5
Morland Cl DUN/HR/TOD LU5 ....40 C5
Morrell Cl LTNN/LIM LU3 ....33 C1
Morris Cl LTNN/LIM LU3 ....33 C3
Mortimer Cl LTN LU1 ....44 A5
Mossbank Av LTNW/LEA LU4 ......45 C3
Mossdale Ct LTNW/LEA LU4 *.....32 C5
Mossman Dr LTN LU1 ....44 A5
Mostyn Rd LTNW/LEA LU4 ....33 E4
Moulton Ri LTNE LU2 ....44 C1
Mountfield Rd LTNE LU2 ....44 C1
Mount Grace Rd LTNE LU2 ....55 C2
Mount Pleasant Av
  DUN/HR/TOD LU5 ....20 B1
Mount Pleasant Rd
  LTNN/LIM LU3 ....33 E3
The Mount LTNE LU2 ....33 H1
Mountview Av
  DUN/HR/TOD LU5 ....41 F5
Moxes Wd LTNN/LIM LU3 ....33 E1
Muirfield LTNE LU2 ....34 C2
Mulberry Cl LTNN/LIM LU3 ....33 F4
Mulberry Pl STALW/RED AL3 *.....71 F3
Mullion Cl LTNE LU2 ....43 F2
Muscat Cl LTNW/LEA LU4 * 43 F2
Mussons Pth LTNE LU2 ....45 H2
Muswell Cl LTNN/LIM LU3 ....33 H2
Mutford Cft LTNE LU2 ....45 H2

N

Nairn Cl HARP AL5 ....73 F1
Napier Rd LTN LU1 ....4 A5
Nappsbury Rd LTNW/LEA LU4 ....32 D5

Naseby Rd LTN LU1 ....43 H4
Nash Cl DUN/HR/TOD LU5 ....31 F3
Nayland Cl LTNE LU2 ....46 A2
Needham Rd LTNW/LEA LU4 ......32 B2
Nethercott Cl LTNE LU2 ....45 G2
Netherfield Rd HARP AL5 ....72 D5
Nettle Cl LTNW/LEA LU4 ....33 C3
Neville Rd LTNN/LIM LU3 ....33 C3
Newark Rd LTNW/LEA LU4 ....43 G1
New Bedford Rd
  LTNN/LIM LU3 ....34 B5
Newbold Rd LTNN/LIM LU3 ....31 H3
Newbury Cl LTNW/LEA LU4 ....43 E1
Newbury Rd DUN/HR/TOD LU5...31 C2
Newcombe Rd LTN LU1 ....44 A4
New Fiddlers HI HARP AL5 *.........63 C4
Newlands Rd
  AMP/FLIT/BLC MK45 ....7 G2
  LTN LU1 ....54 B4
Newmans Dr HARP AL5 ....68 B2
Newnham Cl LTNE LU2 ....45 H2
New St LTN LU1 ....4 B6
  LTN LU1 ....54 A5
Newton Cl HARP AL5 ....73 F1
Newtondale LTNW/LEA LU4 ....32 C3
New Town Rd LTNE LU2 ....4 D7
New Town St LTN LU1 ....4 D7
New Woodfield Gn
  DUN/HR/TOD LU5 ....41 G5
Nicholas Wy DUN/WHIP LU6 *......2 B2
Nichols Cl AMP/FLIT/BLC MK45.....9 H4
  STALW/RED AL3 ....70 D2
Nichols Cl LTNE LU2 ....45 F1
Nightingale Cl LTNE LU2 ....35 C2
Nightingale Cl LTNW/LEA LU4 *...45 H2
Nine Lands LBUZ LU7 ....19 D3
Ninth Av LTNN/LIM LU3 ....32 D1
Noke Shot HARP AL5 ....65 E5
Norcott Cl DUN/HR/TOD LU5 ......3 C6
Norfolk Rd DUN/HR/TOD LU5 .....41 G5
Norman Rd
  AMP/FLIT/BLC MK45 ....10 A4
  LTNN/LIM LU3 ....43 H1
Norman Wy DUN/WHIP LU6 ....40 A3
Northall Cl DUN/WHIP LU6 ....38 B5
Northall Rd DUN/WHIP LU6 ....48 B1
Northcliffe DUN/WHIP LU6 ....38 C5
North Common Rd
  STALW/RED AL3 ....71 E3
North Drift Wy LTN LU1 ....43 H5
Northfield Rd HARP AL5 ....65 E5
Northfields DUN/HR/TOD LU5 .....30 B5
North Station Wy
  DUN/WHIP LU6 ....40 B2
North St LTNE LU2 ....4 D1
Northview Rd
  DUN/HR/TOD LU5 ....40 C1
  LTN LU1 ....44 D1
Northwell Dr LTNN/LIM LU3 ....23 F5
Norton Rd LTNN/LIM LU3 ....33 F4
Nunnery La LTNN/LIM LU3 ....33 H3
The Nurseries DUN/WHIP LU6 ....38 C5
Nursery Cl DUN/WHIP LU6 ....2 A4
Nursery Pde LTNN/LIM LU3 ....33 H4
Nursery Rd LTNN/LIM LU3 ....33 H4
Nymans Cl LTNE LU2 ....35 H5

O

Oak Cl AMP/FLIT/BLC MK45 ....7 G1
  DUN/HR/TOD LU5 ....3 C5
  DUN/HR/TOD LU5 ....13 H1
Oakfield Rd HARP AL5 ....72 C2
Oakhurst Av HARP AL5 ....72 B1
Oakley Cl LTNW/LEA LU4 ....45 E5
Oakley Rd HARP AL5 ....69 F5
  LTNE LU2 ....32 D4
Oak Rd LTN LU1 ....44 A3
The Oaks LTN LU1 ....54 A5
Oakway DUN/WHIP LU6 ....48 C5
Oak Wy HARP AL5 ....72 C2
Oakwell Cl DUN/HR/TOD LU5......40 B4
Oakwood Av DUN/HR/TOD LU5 ....5 J7
Oakwood Dr HARP AL5 ....72 B2
  LTNN/LIM LU3 ....22 C5
Oatfield Cl LTNW/LEA LU4 ....31 H4
Oban Ter LTN LU1 ....54 B1
Offley Hl HTCH/STOT SG5 ....27 E2
Old Bedford Rd LTNE LU2 ....4 B5
Old Dairy Cl DUN/HR/TOD LU5 ...41 H1
Old Dairy Ct DUN/HR/TOD LU5 ...41 H1
Oldhill DUN/WHIP LU6 ....41 E5
Old Orch LTN LU1 ....54 B1
Old Rectory Cl HARP AL5 ....68 C2
Old Rd AMP/FLIT/BLC MK45 ....16 A1
Old School Ct DUN/WHIP LU6 .....38 D5
Old School Gdns
  AMP/FLIT/BLC MK45 ....10 A5
Old Vicarage Gdns
  STALW/RED AL3 ....60 D4
Old Watling St STALW/RED AL3...61 H5
Olma Rd DUN/HR/TOD LU5 ....40 C1
Olyard Ct LTN LU1 ....53 H1
Onslow Rd LTNW/LEA LU4 ....23 E4
Orchard Av HARP AL5 ....68 B3
Orchard Cl
  AMP/FLIT/BLC MK45 ....16 A1
  DUN/HR/TOD LU5 ....12 B4
  DUN/HR/TOD LU5 ....30 D5
  LTNE LU2 ....53 E2
Orchard End DUN/WHIP LU6 ....48 C2
The Orchards DUN/WHIP LU6 .....38 C5
Orchard La HARP AL5 ....54 A4
Orchard Wy DUN/WHIP LU6 ....48 D1
  HTCHE/RSTV SG4 ....47 G2
  LBUZ LU7 ....28 B3
  LTNE LU2 ....54 C1
Orchid Cl DUN/HR/TOD LU5 ....40 A2
Oregon Wy LTNN/LIM LU3 ....33 C1
Ormsby Cl LTNE LU2 ....54 C1

Orpington Cl LTNW/LEA LU4 ....32 A5
Osborne Rd DUN/WHIP LU6 ....2 C6
  LTN LU1 ....5 F7
Osborn Rd
  AMP/FLIT/BLC MK45 ....10 B4
Otterton Cl HARP AL5 ....68 B1
Oulton Ri HARP AL5 ....68 B1
Ouseley Cl LTNW/LEA LU4 ....32 D5
Overfield Rd HARP AL5 ....45 G2
Overstone Rd HARP AL5 ....69 E3
  LTNE LU2 ....42 D2
Owing Cl LTNW/LEA LU4 ....45 H1
Oxen Rd LTNE LU2 ....33 H1
Oxford Rd HTCHE/RSTV SG4 ....11 H4
  LTN LU1 ....4 D6
Ox La HARP AL5 ....68 D1

P

Packhorse Pl DUN/WHIP LU6 ....60 C1
Paddock Cl LTNW/LEA LU4 ....31 H4
Paddock Wy LTNE LU2 *...............35 H4
Paddock Wd HARP AL5 ....60 C5
Paignton Cl LTNW/LEA LU4 ....32 D4
Palma Cl DUN/WHIP LU6 ....30 B5
The Parade DUN/WHIP LU6 ....2 B2
Park Av DUN/HR/TOD LU5 ....31 E3
  DUN/WHIP LU6 ....30 B5
  LTN/LIM LU3 ....32 C1
Park Av North HARP AL5 ....68 B3
Park Av South HARP AL5 ....68 A3
Parkdale HARP AL5 ....60 D4
Parkfield STALW/RED AL3 ....60 D4
Park Hi DUN/HR/TOD LU5 ....12 B3
  HARP AL5 ....68 B2
Parkland Dr HARP AL5 ....54 B1
Park La DUN/WHIP LU6 ....38 B5
Park Leys DUN/HR/TOD LU5 ....13 H1
Park Meadow Cl
  AMP/FLIT/BLC MK45 ....9 H4
Park Mt HARP AL5 ....68 A2
Park Ri HARP AL5 ....68 A1
Park Rise Cl HARP AL5 ....68 A1
Park Rd AMP/FLIT/BLC MK45 ....7 G2
  DUN/HR/TOD LU5 ....3 F6
  DUN/HR/TOD LU5 ....12 A3
Park Rd North
  DUN/HR/TOD LU5 ....31 E4
Parkside Cl DUN/HR/TOD LU5 ....31 F3
Parkside Dr DUN/HR/TOD LU5 ....31 F3
Park Sq LTNE LU2 ....2 B2
  LTN LU1 ....4 D6
Park St West LTN LU1 ....4 D6
Park Ter LTN LU1 ....4 E6
The Park STALW/RED AL3 ....71 F3
Park Viad LTN LU1 ....4 E6
Park View Cl LTNW/LEA LU4 ....32 D2
Park View Dr STALW/RED AL3.....60 D5
Parkview La LBUZ LU7 ....19 D3
Parrot Cl LTNN/LIM LU3 ....5 J3
Partridge Cl LTNW/LEA LU4 ....32 A3
Parva Cl HARP AL5 ....73 F1
Parys Rd LTNN/LIM LU3 ....33 H2
Pascomb Rd DUN/WHIP LU6 ....40 B3
Pasture La HTCHE/RSTV SG4 ....47 G3
The Pastures DUN/WHIP LU6 ......48 D3
Pastures Wy LTNW/LEA LU4 ....31 H3
Patterdale Cl LTNN/LIM LU3 ....2 C2
Peach Cl LTNE LU2 ....4 E6
Peartree Cl LTNW/LEA LU4 ....12 A5
Peartree Rd LTNE LU2 ....4 E6
Pebblemoor DUN/WHIP LU6 ....48 D3
Peck Ct AMP/FLIT/BLC MK45 ....9 H3
Peddars La LBUZ LU7 ....28 B4
Peel Pl LTN LU1 ....4 B5
Peel St DUN/HR/TOD LU5 ....50 D5
  LTN LU1 ....54 A5
Pegsdon Cl LTNN/LIM LU3 ....33 H1
Pegsdon Wy HTCH/STOT SG5 .....17 H1
Pembroke Av LTNW/LEA LU4 ......33 E5
Penda Cl LTNN/LIM LU3 ....33 F2
Pendennis Ct HARP AL5 ....54 A4
Penhill LTNN/LIM LU3 ....33 H3
Pennine Av LTNN/LIM LU3 ....22 C5
Penny Cft HARP AL5 ....72 C3
Penrith Av DUN/WHIP LU6 ....2 D6
Penshurst Cl HARP AL5 ....63 H5
Pepsal End Rd LTN LU1 ....62 A3
Percheron Dr LTNW/LEA LU4 ......32 A3
Percival Wy LTNE LU2 ....45 G4
Peregrine Rd LTNW/LEA LU4 ....32 A4
Periwinkle La DUN/WHIP LU6 *....3 F6
Periwinkle Ter DUN/WHIP LU6 *...3 F6
Perry Mead DUN/WHIP LU6 ....48 C1
Perrymead LTNE LU2 ....46 B1
Petard Cl LTNW/LEA LU4 ....42 A1
Petersfield Gdns
  LTNN/LIM LU3 ....23 E4
Petunia Ct LTNW/LEA LU4 ....44 A2
Pevensey Cl LTNE LU2 ....35 H4
Pickford HI HARP AL5 ....68 C1
Pie Cnr STALW/RED AL3 ....66 A3
Pie Gdn STALW/RED AL3 ....66 A3
Pigeonwick HARP AL5 ....68 C1
Piggottshill La HARP AL5 ....69 F4
Pightle Cl LTNW/LEA LU4 ....32 D4
Pilgrims Cl DUN/HR/TOD LU5 .....13 H2
Pinewood Cl LTNN/LIM LU3 ....22 C4
Pinford Dell LTNE LU2 ....45 H2
Pipers Av HARP AL5 ....69 F5
Pipers Cl STALW/RED AL3 ....71 E1
Pipers Cft DUN/WHIP LU6 ....40 B4
Pipers La HARP AL5 ....68 B1
  STALW/RED AL3 ....61 E1
Pirton Rd LTNW/LEA LU4 ....32 C3
Plaiters Wy DUN/WHIP LU6 ....30 C3
Plantation Rd LTNE LU2 ....32 D1
Platt Cl LTNW/LEA LU4 ....32 C4
Playford Sq LTNW/LEA LU4 *.......32 D4
The Pleasance HARP AL5 ....63 H5
Plewes Cl DUN/WHIP LU6 ....59 G1
Plough Cl LTNW/LEA LU4 ....31 G4

Plough Ct LTNW/LEA LU4 *..........31 G4
Plummers La LTNE LU2 ....57 F5
Plumpton Cl LTNE LU2 ....35 H5
Plymouth Cl LTN LU1 ....5 E1
Poets Ct HARP AL5 ....68 D8
Polegate Cl LTNW/LEA LU4 ....42 A1
Polegate Cl LTNE LU2 ....34 C3
Polzeath Cl LTNE LU2 ....45 G3
Pomeroy Gv LTNE LU2 ....34 C3
Pomfret Av LTNE LU2 ....5 F2
Pond Cl LTNW/LEA LU4 ....32 B3
Pondsmeade STALW/RED AL3.....71 F2
Pondwick Rd HARP AL5 ....68 A2
Pondwicks Rd LTN LU1 ....5 F4
Poplar Av LTNN/LIM LU3 ....24 A5
Poplar Rd DUN/WHIP LU6 ....59 G1
Poplars Cl LTNE LU2 ....35 F5
Porlock Dr LTNE LU2 ....45 G2
Porters HI HARP AL5 ....65 E5
Portland Cl DUN/HR/TOD LU5 ....50 D5
Portland St LTNW/LEA LU4 ....43 G2
Portland Rd LTNW/LEA LU4 ....43 G2
Portobello Cl
  AMP/FLIT/BLC MK45 ....10 A5
Porz Av DUN/HR/TOD LU5 ....31 F4
Pottery Cl LTNN/LIM LU3 ....33 F1
The Pound AMP/FLIT/BLC MK45....7 G1
Power Ct LTN LU1 ....5 F4
Poynings Cl HARP AL5 ....69 H4
Poynters Rd DUN/HR/TOD LU5 ...31 G5
Prebendal Dr LTNE LU2 ....33 H3
Prentice Wy LTNE LU2 ....45 H4
President Wy LTNE LU2 ....44 D1
Preston Gdns LTNE LU2 ....44 D1
Preston Pth LTNE LU2 ....44 D1
Preston Rd DUN/HR/TOD LU5 ....12 C5
Prestwick Cl LTNE LU2 ....34 C5
Priestleys LTN LU1 ....43 G4
Princess St LTN LU1 ....4 B6
Princes St DUN/HR/TOD LU5 ......12 B5
  DUN/WHIP LU6 ....2 B4
Prince Wy LTNE LU2 ....45 H3
Printers Wy DUN/WHIP LU6 ....2 B4
Priory Gdns LTNE LU2 ....34 B5
Priory Rd DUN/HR/TOD LU5 ....2 E4
The Priory STALW/RED AL3 * 71 F2
Proctor Wy LTNE LU2 ....45 G4
Progress Pk LTNW/LEA LU4 ....32 B1
Progress Wy LTNW/LEA LU4 ....32 B1
Prospect La HARP AL5 ....72 B3
Prospect Wy LTNE LU2 ....45 G4
Provost Wy LTNE LU2 ....45 H4
Prudence Cl DUN/HR/TOD LU5 ...13 G1
Purcell Rd LTNW/LEA LU4 ....2 A4
Purway Cl LTNN/LIM LU3 ....23 E5
Putteridge Bde LTNE LU2 *..........35 F4
Putteridge Rd LTNE LU2 ....35 F4
The Pyghtle
  AMP/FLIT/BLC MK45 ....9 G2
  LTN LU1 ....43 G4
Pynders La DUN/HR/TOD LU5 ......3 K1
Pytchley Cl LTNE LU2 ....34 C3

Q

The Quadrant
  DUN/HR/TOD LU5 ....31 E3
Quantock Cl LTNN/LIM LU3 ....23 H5
Quantock Cl LTNN/LIM LU3 ....23 H5
Quantock Ri LTNN/LIM LU3 ....23 H5
Quarry Wy DUN/WHIP LU6...........2 A7
Queens Rd HARP AL5 ....68 D5
Queen St DUN/HR/TOD LU5 ....30 D4
Queensway DUN/WHIP LU6 ....2 D3
Queensway Pde DUN/WHIP LU6....2 D3
Quickswood LTNN/LIM LU3 ....33 G1
Quilter Cl LTNN/LIM LU3 ....33 F4

R

Rackman Dr LTNN/LIM LU3 ....34 A3
Radburn Ct LTNW/LEA LU4 ....2 A3
Radnor Rd LTNW/LEA LU4 ....31 H4
Radstone Pl LTNE LU2 ....46 A2
Raglan Cl LTNW/LEA LU4 * 31 H5
Rainbow Ct DUN/HR/TOD LU5 ....70 D2
Raleigh Gv LTNW/LEA LU4 ....42 D2
Ramridge Rd LTNE LU2 ....45 E1
Ramsey Cl LTNN/LIM LU3 ....31 H5
Ramsey Rd
  AMP/FLIT/BLC MK45 ....10 A4
Randall Dr DUN/HR/TOD LU5......20 B1
Ranleigh Wk HARP AL5 ....73 F1
Ranock Cl LTNN/LIM LU3 ....22 D5
Ravenbank Rd LTNN/LIM LU3 ......33 G1
Ravenhill Wy LTNW/LEA LU4 ......32 A4
Ravensburgh Cl
  AMP/FLIT/BLC MK45 ....9 H4
Ravenscourt DUN/WHIP LU6 ....30 B5
Ravenscroft HARP AL5 ....73 F1
Ravensthorpe LTNE LU2 ....35 H2
Raynham Wy LTNE LU2 ....45 H2
Readers Cl DUN/WHIP LU6 ....2 A4
Reaper Cl LTNW/LEA LU4 ....31 G4
Recreation Rd
  DUN/HR/TOD LU5 ....31 E2
Rectory La LTNE LU2 ....25 H3
Redbournbury La
  STALW/RED AL3 ....71 H5
Redbourn La HARP AL5 ....72 A1
Redding La STALW/RED AL3.........66 C5
Redferns Cl LTNE LU2 ....35 H4
Redfield Cl DUN/HR/TOD LU5 .....40 A2
Redgrave Gdns LTNN/LIM LU3 ....23 F5
Redmire Cl LTNW/LEA LU4 ....32 B2
Red Rails LTN LU1 ....53 C5
Redwood Dr LTNN/LIM LU3 ....22 C5
Reed Pl HARP AL5 *.....................68 B1
Reedsdale LTNE LU2 ....46 B1

Reeves Av LTNN/LIM LU3
Regency St DUN/WHIP LU6
Regent St DUN/WHIP LU6
  LTN LU1 *
Reginald St LTNE LU2
Regis Rd LTNW/LEA LU4
Renshaw Cl LTNE LU2
Repton Cl LTNW/LEA LU4
The Retreat DUN/HR/TOD LU5
Ribocon Wy LTNW/LEA LU4
Richards Cl LTN LU1
Richard St DUN/HR/TOD LU5
Richmond Hl LTNE LU2
Richmond Rd
  AMP/FLIT/BLC MK45
Rickyard Cl LTN LU1
Rickyard Meadow
  STALW/RED AL3
Riddy La LTNN/LIM LU3
The Ride DUN/WHIP LU6
Ridge Av HARP AL5
Ridgedown STALW/RED AL3
Ridgeway DUN/WHIP LU6
  HARP AL5 *
Ridgeway Av DUN/HR/TOD LU5
Ridgeway Dr DUN/HR/TOD LU5
Ridgewood Dr HARP AL5
Ridgeway Gdns HARP AL5
Ridgway Rd LTNE LU2
The Ridings LTNN/LIM LU3
  STALW/RED AL3
Ringwood Rd LTNE LU2
Ripley Rd LTNW/LEA LU4
Riverford Cl HARP AL5
Riverside Rd LTNN/LIM LU3
River Wy LTNN/LIM LU3
Robin Cl HARP AL5
Robinson Crs DUN/HR/TOD LU5
Robinswood LTNE LU2
Rochester Av LTNE LU2
Rochford Dr LTNE LU2
Rockley Rd LTN LU1
Rodeheath LTNW/LEA LU4
Rodney Cl LTNW/LEA LU4
Roebuck Cl LTN LU1
Roedean Cl LTNE LU2
Roe End La STALW/RED AL3
Rogate Rd LTNE LU2
Roman Gdns DUN/HR/TOD LU5
Roman Rd
  AMP/FLIT/BLC MK45
  LTNW/LEA LU4
Roman Wy DUN/HR/TOD LU5
Rondini Av LTNE LU2
Rookery Dr LTNE LU2
Ropkins Cl AMP/FLIT/BLC MK45
Rosebery Av HARP AL5
Rose Ct DUN/WHIP LU6 *
Rosedale DUN/HR/TOD LU5
Rosedale Cl LTNW/LEA LU4
Rose Wk DUN/HR/TOD LU5
  HARP AL5
Rose Wood Cl LTNE LU2
Roslyn Wy DUN/HR/TOD LU5
Ross Cl LTN LU1
Rossfold Rd LTNN/LIM LU3
Rosslyn Crs LTNN/LIM LU3
Rossway LTN LU1
Rothamsted Av HARP AL5
Rotheram Av LTNE LU2
Rother Fld LTNE LU2
Rotherwood Cl DUN/WHIP LU6
Rothesay Rd LTN LU1
Roundfield Av HARP AL5
Roundwood Gdns HARP AL5
Roundwood La HARP AL5
Roundwood Pk HARP AL5
Rowan Av LTN LU1
Rowan Wy HARP AL5
Rowelfield LTNE LU2
Rowington Cl LTNE LU2
Royal London Mt LTN LU1 *
Royal Wk DUN/HR/TOD LU5
Royce Cl DUN/WHIP LU6
Roydon Cl LTNW/LEA LU4
Rudyard Ct LTNW/LEA LU4
Rueley Dell Rd LTNE LU2
The Ruins STALW/RED AL3
Runfold Av LTNN/LIM LU3
Runham Cl LTNW/LEA LU4
Runley Rd LTN LU1
Runnymede Ct LTNN/LIM LU3 *
Rushall Gn LTNE LU2
Rusper Gn LTNE LU2
Russell Cl DUN/WHIP LU6
Russell Ms LTNE LU2 *
Russell Ri LTN LU1
Russell Rd DUN/HR/TOD LU5
Ruthin Cl LTN LU1
Rutland Crs LTNE LU2
Rydal Wy LTNN/LIM LU3
Ryde Cl LTN LU1 *
Ryecroft Wy LTNE LU2
Ryefield LTNN/LIM LU3
Rye Hl HARP AL5
Rylands Heath LTNE LU2
Ryton Cl LTN LU1

S

Saberton Cl STALW/RED AL3
Sacombe Gn LTNN/LIM LU3
Saffron Cl LTNE LU2
Saffron Rd DUN/HR/TOD LU5
St Albans Rd HARP AL5
  STALW/RED AL3
St Andrew's Av HARP AL5
St Andrew's Ct LTN LU1
St Andrews La
  DUN/HR/TOD LU5

Whitecroft Rd *LTNE* LU2 .....5 G3
Whitefield Av *LTNE* LU2 .....32 C1
Whitehaven *LTNN/LIM* LU5 .....23 F4
Whitehill Av *LTN* LU1 .....54 B1
White Hill Rd
  AMP/FLIT/BLC MK45 .....10 A4
White Horse Cl *LBUZ* LU7 .....18 C3
Whitehorse V *LTNN/LIM* LU5 .....23 F4
Whitehouse Cl
  DUN/HR/TOD LU5 .....30 D4
Whitethorn Wy *LTN* LU1 .....43 G5
Whitewaybottom La *LTNE* LU2 .....47 H5
Whitings Cl *HARP* AL5 .....65 F5
Whittingham Cl *LTNE* LU2 .....46 B2
Whitwell Cl *LTNN/LIM* LU5 .....23 H5
The Wickets *LTNE* LU2 .....44 B2
Wick Hl *DUN/WHIP* LU6 .....59 H1
Wickmere Cl *LTNE* LU2 .....34 A1
Wickstead Av *LTNW/LEA* LU4 .....33 E5
Wigmore La *LTNE* LU2 .....35 F5
Wigmore Pl *LTNE* LU2 .....46 A2
Wilbury Dr *DUN/HR/TOD* LU5 .....41 G1
Wild Cherry Dr *LTN* LU1 * 54 B1
Willenhall Cl *LTNN/LIM* LU5 .....33 C1
William St *LTNE* LU2 .....4 C1
  STALW/RED AL3 .....61 E4

Williton Rd *LTNE* LU2 .....45 F1
Willoughby Cl *DUN/WHIP* LU6 .....3 F7
Willoughby Rd *HARP* AL5 .....64 D5
The Willows *DUN/WHIP* LU6 .....48 D5
Willow Wy *DUN/HR/TOD* LU5 .....12 B5
  HARP AL5 .....65 E5
  LTNN/LIM LU3 .....33 E3
Wilsden Av *LTN* LU1 .....44 A5
Wimborne Rd *LTN* LU1 .....43 H3
Wimple Rd *LTNW/LEA* LU4 .....42 A1
Winchester Gdns
  LTNN/LIM LU3 .....23 E4
Winchfield *LTN* LU1 .....53 E2
Winch St *LTNE* LU2 .....44 D2
Windermere Cl *DUN/WHIP* LU6 .....2 C6
Windermere Crs *LTNN/LIM* LU3 .....33 F3
Windmill Rd *HTCHE/RSTV* SG4 .....47 F1
  LTNE LU2 .....5 F6
  LTN LU1 .....61 G5
Windsor Dr *DUN/HR/TOD* LU5 .....31 F4
Windsor Pde
  AMP/FLIT/BLC MK45 * 10 A3
Windsor Rd
  AMP/FLIT/BLC MK45 .....10 A3
Windsor St *LTN* LU1 .....4 B7
Windsor Wk *LTN* LU1 .....4 B6

Winfield St *DUN/WHIP* LU6 .....2 C3
Wingate Rd *DUN/HR/TOD* LU5 .....3 K2
  HARP AL5 .....65 H5
LTNW/LEA LU4 .....45 F1
Wingfield Rd *LBUZ* LU7 .....19 G3
Winkfield Cl *LTNW/LEA* LU4 .....42 B2
Winsdon Rd *LTN* LU1 .....4 A6
Winslow Cl *LTNN/LIM* LU3 .....34 A4
Winston Cl *LTNE* LU2 .....34 B2
Wiseman Cl *LTNE* LU2 .....34 B2
Wistow Rd *LTNN/LIM* LU3 .....33 G2
Withy Cl *LTNW/LEA* LU4 .....32 B3
Wivelsfield *DUN/WHIP* LU6 .....38 C5
Wiveton Cl *LTNE* LU2 .....34 B1
Woburn Rd *LBUZ* LU7 .....18 C5
Woodcroft Rd *LTNN/LIM* LU3 .....33 H2
Woodcock Rd *LTN* LU1 .....44 A5
Wood End Hl *HARP* AL5 .....67 H1
Wood End Rd *HARP* AL5 .....67 H1
Woodfield Ga
  DUN/WHIP LU6 .....41 G5

Woodford Rd *DUN/HR/TOD* LU5 .....3 K2
Wood Green Cl *LTNE* LU2 .....35 F5
Wood Green Rd *LTNE* LU2 .....35 F5
Woodland Av *LTNN/LIM* LU3 .....43 H1
Woodland Ri *DUN/WHIP* LU6 .....58 D2
Woodlands *HARP* AL5 .....68 A1
  LBUZ LU7 .....19 G3
  LTN LU1 .....53 E4
Woodlands Av
  DUN/HR/TOD LU5 .....51 E4
Woodmere *LTNN/LIM* LU3 .....23 G4
Woodside *DUN/WHIP* LU6 .....38 C5
Woodside Pk
  DUN/HR/TOD LU5 .....51 E5
Woodside Rd *LTN* LU1 .....53 G5
Wood St *DUN/WHIP* LU6 .....2 E5
  HARP AL5 .....1 E7
Woolams *STALW/RED* AL3 * 71 E3
Woollams *STALW/RED* AL3 * 71 E3
Woolpack Cl *DUN/WHIP* LU6 .....2 E6
Wootton Cl *LTNN/LIM* LU3 .....53 H2
Wordsworth Rd *HARP* AL5 .....68 C1
Worthington Rd
  DUN/WHIP LU6 .....40 B3
Wraysbury Cl *LTNW/LEA* LU4 .....32 D5

Wren Cl *LTNE* LU2
Wren Wk *DUN/WHIP* LU6
Wroxham Wy *HARP* AL5
Wulwards Cl *LTN* LU1
Wychwood Av *LTNE* LU2
Wycliffe Cl *LTNN/LIM* LU3
Wycombe Wy *LTNW/LEA* LU4
Wyken Cl *LTNN/LIM* LU3
Wyndham Rd *LTNW/LEA* LU4
Wyvern Cl *LTNW/LEA* LU4

Y

Yately Cl *LTNE* LU2
Yeomans Av *HARP* AL5
Yeovil Rd *LTN* LU1
Yew St *DUN/HR/TOD* LU5
Yew Tree Cl *DUN/WHIP* LU6
York Cl *AMP/FLIT/BLC* MK45
York St *LTNE* LU2

Index - featured places

Abbeygate Business Centre
  LTNE LU2 .....4 E3
Airport Executive
  Industrial Park *LTNE* LU2 .....45 H3
Aldwickbury Park Golf Club
  HARP AL5 .....69 G3
Allied Business Centre
  HARP AL5 .....69 E1
Apex Business Centre
  DUN/HR/TOD LU5 .....41 E1
Ardley Hill Lower School
  DUN/WHIP LU6 .....41 E5
Arianne Business Centre
  DUN/HR/TOD LU5 .....40 D1
Arndale Shopping Centre
  LTN LU1 .....4 C4
Arnold Middle School
  AMP/FLIT/BLC MK45 .....10 B5
Ascot Business Centre
  LTN LU1 .....4 A5
Ashcroft High School
  LTNE LU2 .....45 G1
Ashton Middle School
  DUN/WHIP LU6 .....2 C2
Ashton St Peters VA
  Lower School
  DUN/HR/TOD LU5 .....2 E3
Asquith Court School
  HARP AL5 .....68 B1
Barnfield College
  LTN LU1 .....53 H1
  LTNE LU2 .....34 B3
Barnfield College Technology
  Centre
  LTNN/LIM LU3 .....23 H5
Barratt Industrial Park
  LTNE LU2 .....45 G4
Barton Hills Nature Reserve
  LTNE LU2 .....16 B4
Barton Industrial Estate
  AMP/FLIT/BLC MK45 .....9 G3
Barton Rovers FC
  AMP/FLIT/BLC MK45 .....10 A5
Beech Hill Community
  Primary School
  LTNW/LEA LU4 .....43 H2
Beechwood J & I School
  LTNW/LEA LU4 .....33 E4
Beecroft Lower School
  DUN/WHIP LU6 .....40 B2
The Borough Industrial Estate
  LTN LU1 .....33 G5
Bramingham Business Park
  LTNN/LIM LU3 .....23 H5
Bramingham Park Medical
  Centre *LTNN/LIM* LU3 .....23 G5
Bramingham Park Study Centre
  LTNN/LIM LU3 .....23 H5
Bramingham Primary School
  LTNN/LIM LU3 .....23 H4
Breachwood Green
  Primary School
  HTCHE/RSTV SG4 .....47 G2
Brewers Hill Middle School
  DUN/WHIP LU6 .....40 A2
Broadmead School
  LTN LU1 .....54 C1
Broomstick Industrial Estate
  DUN/WHIP LU6 .....48 C2
Bushmead Primary School
  LTNE LU2 .....34 C3
Caddington Sports Club
  LTN LU1 .....55 F3
Cardinal Newman School
  LTNE LU2 .....24 A4
Chalgrave Manor Golf Club
  DUN/HR/TOD LU5 .....20 C3
Chalney Community College
  LTNW/LEA LU4 .....32 C5
Chalton Lower School
  LTNW/LEA LU4 .....21 G4
Chantry J & I School
  LTNW/LEA LU4 .....31 H4
Cheynes Infant School
  LTNN/LIM LU3 .....22 D5
Chiltern FM
  DUN/WHIP LU6 .....2 A2
The Chiltern Hotel
  LTNW/LEA LU4 .....43 F1

Chiltern Park
  Industrial Estate
  DUN/HR/TOD LU5 .....3 G1
Cineworld Cinema *LTN* LU1 .....4 B3
Circle Business Centre
  LTN LU1 .....30 C5
Cockernhoe Endowed
  Primary School *LTNE* LU2 .....36 B4
Commonwealth College
  LTN LU1 .....4 B5
Cotswold Business Park
  LTN LU1 .....52 D4
Crabtree J & I School
  LTNW/LEA LU4 .....69 E3
Crawley Green Infant School
  LTNE LU2 .....5 J3
Dallow Community Primary
  School *LTN* LU1 .....44 A3
Dallow Junior School
  LTN LU1 .....44 A3
Dalroad Industrial Estate
  LTN LU1 .....43 H3
Denbigh High School
  LTNN/LIM LU3 .....44 A1
Denbigh J & I School
  LTN LU1 .....43 H1
Downside J & I School
  LTNW/LEA LU4 .....43 E2
Downside Lower School
  LTN LU1 .....43 J6
Dukeminster Trading Estate
  DUN/HR/TOD LU5 .....3 F5
Dunstable College
  DUN/HR/TOD LU5 .....2 E2
Dunstable Downs Country
  Park *DUN/WHIP* LU6 .....50 B2
Dunstable Downs Golf Club
  DUN/WHIP LU6 .....50 B1
Dunstable FC
  DUN/WHIP LU6 .....40 B1
Dunstable Health Centre
  DUN/HR/TOD LU5 .....2 E4
Dunstable Icknield
  Lower School
  DUN/WHIP LU6 .....2 C5
Dunstable Leisure Centre
  DUN/WHIP LU6 .....2 C5
Dunstable Road Infant School
  LTN LU1 .....44 A3
Dunstable Town CC
  DUN/WHIP LU6 .....39 G4
Dunstablians RUFC
  DUN/HR/TOD LU5 .....30 C2
Eastern Avenue
  Industrial Estate
  DUN/HR/TOD LU5 .....3 H4
Eaton Bray Lower School
  DUN/WHIP LU6 .....38 C5
Edlesborough School
  DUN/WHIP LU6 .....48 C3
Elliswick Lawn Tennis Club
  HARP AL5 .....68 D2
Express by Holiday Inn
  LTNE LU2 .....45 H5
  STALW/RED AL3 .....61 G5
Farley Junior School
  LTN LU1 .....54 A1
Ferrars J & I School
  LTNW/LEA LU4 .....32 B5
Firbank Industrial Estate
  LTN LU1 .....43 G3
Five Oaks Middle School
  LTN LU1 .....53 F3
Flowers Industrial Estate
  LTN LU1 .....4 D6
Foxdell Infant School
  LTN LU1 .....43 G3
Foxdell Junior School
  LTN LU1 .....43 E3
Galaxy Leisure Centre
  LTN LU1 .....4 B3
Glenwood School
  LTNW/LEA LU4 .....51 G1
Gooseberry Hill Health Centre
  LTNN/LIM LU3 .....33 H1
The Greenhouse Health Centre
  LTN LU1 .....4 A3
Griffin Golf Club
  LTN LU1 .....42 D5

The Grove Infant School
  HARP AL5 .....69 F4
The Grove Junior School
  HARP AL5 .....69 F4
Guardian Industrial Estate
  LTN LU1 .....44 A3
GX Superbowl
  DUN/HR/TOD LU5 .....2 D2
Hadrian Lower School
  DUN/HR/TOD LU5 .....3 J1
Halyard High School
  LTNW/LEA LU4 .....31 H5
Hanover International Hotel
  LTNE LU2 .....2 E4
  HARP AL5 .....68 C2
Harlington Lower School
  LTNE LU2 .....7 H5
Harlington Upper School
  LTNE LU2 .....8 A4
Harpenden Common Golf Club
  HARP AL5 .....72 D1
Harpenden Golf Club
  HARP AL5 .....72 B2
Harpenden Health Centre
  HARP AL5 .....68 C2
Harpenden Hospital
  HARP AL5 .....64 C5
Harpenden House Hotel
  HARP AL5 .....68 D4
Harpenden Memorial Hospital
  HARP AL5 .....68 D2
Harpenden Preparatory School
  HARP AL5 .....68 B2
Harpenden RUFC
  HARP AL5 .....72 A1
Harpenden Sports Centre
  HARP AL5 .....68 C4
Harpenden Swimming Pool
  HARP AL5 .....68 C3
Hart Hill Primary School
  LTNE LU2 .....5 F2
Hawthorn Park Lower School
  DUN/HR/TOD LU5 .....31 F2
Heathfield Lower School
  LTN LU1 .....53 E2
Heron Trading Estate
  LTNN/LIM LU3 .....32 C1
Herts County Agricultural
  Showground
  STALW/RED AL3 .....66 C3
Hexton Primary School
  HTCH/STOT SG5 .....17 E1
High Beeches Primary School
  HARP AL5 .....69 F4
Hillborough J & I School
  LTN LU1 .....44 A5
Hillcrest Special School
  LTN LU1 .....3 J2
Hockcliffe Business Centre
  LBUZ LU7 .....18 D4
Hockliffe Lower School
  LBUZ LU7 .....18 C2
Holly Street Trading Estate
  LTN LU1 .....4 C6
Hotel Ibis
  LTN LU1 .....45 G4
Hotel St Lawrence
  LTN LU1 .....4 C4
Houghton Regis Health Centre
  DUN/HR/TOD LU5 .....30 D4
Houghton Regis Lower School
  DUN/HR/TOD LU5 .....30 C4
Houghton Regis
  Medical Centre
  DUN/HR/TOD LU5 .....31 E3
Houghton Regis Trading Centre
  DUN/HR/TOD LU5 .....30 D4
Icknield High School
  Arts College *LTNW/LIM* LU3 .....34 A3
Icknield Primary School
  LTNN/LIM LU3 .....33 H3
Ivinghoe Business Centre
  DUN/HR/TOD LU5 .....30 D5
John Dony Field Centre
  LTNE LU2 .....34 C2
Kensworth Lower School
  DUN/WHIP LU6 .....59 H1
Kings Houghton Middle School
  DUN/HR/TOD LU5 .....31 F1

Kingsland Community College
  DUN/HR/TOD LU5 .....31 G2
The Kings School
  HARP AL5 .....64 B5
Kingsway Industrial Estate
  LTN LU1 .....43 G3
Lady Zia Werner School
  LTNE LU2 .....35 F5
Lancot Lower School
  DUN/WHIP LU6 .....40 A3
Langley Terrace Industrial Park
  LTN LU1 .....4 D7
Lark Rise Lower School
  DUN/WHIP LU6 .....40 D5
Lawrence Industrial Estate
  DUN/WHIP LU6 .....40 D1
Leagrave Health Centre
  LTNW/LEA LU4 .....32 C4
Leagrave J & I School
  LTNW/LEA LU4 .....32 C4
Lea Industrial Estate
  HARP AL5 .....65 E5
Lealands High School
  LTNN/LIM LU3 .....22 C5
Lea Manor High School
  LTNN/LIM LU3 .....23 F5
The Lea Primary School
  HARP AL5 .....64 C5
Lewsey Farm Clinic
  LTNW/LEA LU4 .....31 H4
Library Theatre
  LTN LU1 .....4 C4
The Little Theatre
  DUN/HR/TOD LU5 .....2 E5
Liverpool Road Health Centre
  LTN LU1 .....4 A3
Lodge Clinic
  LTN LU1 .....4 C5
London Luton Airport
  LTNE LU2 .....45 H4
Luton Co-operative Sports Club
  LTNE LU2 .....44 D1
Luton County Court
  LTN LU1 .....4 B4
Luton Crown Court
  LTN LU1 .....4 B4
Luton & Dunstable Hospital
  LTNW/LEA LU4 .....42 C1
Luton Police Station
  LTN LU1 .....4 B5
Luton Retail Park
  LTN LU1 .....5 G7
Luton RUFC *LTN* LU1 .....54 A3
Luton Sixth Form College
  LTNE LU2 .....34 C4
Luton Town FC
  (Kenilworth Rd)
  LTN LU1 .....43 H3
Madrassa Islamic School
  LTNN/LIM LU3 .....44 A2
Maidenhall J & I School
  LTNW/LEA LU4 .....43 G1
Manland Primary School
  HARP AL5 .....68 D1
Manor Farm Business Park
  HTCH/STOT SG5 .....11 E1
Manshead CE School
  DUN/WHIP LU6 .....51 H1
Markyate Primary School
  STALW/RED AL3 .....60 D3
The Meads Primary School
  LTN LU1 .....33 F2
Mill Vale Middle School
  DUN/HR/TOD LU5 .....41 G1
Moorlands School
  LTNW/LEA LU4 .....32 C5
Moreton Park Industrial Estate
  LTNW/LEA LU4 .....32 B1
New Town Trading Estate
  LTN LU1 .....54 C1
The Northfields
  Technology College
  DUN/HR/TOD LU5 .....30 C5
North Luton Industrial Estate
  LTNW/LEA LU4 .....32 B1
Norton Road Primary School
  LTNN/LIM LU3 .....33 H4
Oaklands College
  HARP AL5 .....68 D5

Offley Endowed Primary
  School *HTCH/STOT* SG5 .....2...
Orchard School
  AMP/FLIT/BLC MK45 .....1...
Oxen Industrial Estate
  LTNE LU2 .....5...
Park Avenue Industrial Estate
  LTNE LU2 .....5...
Parkfields Middle School
  DUN/WHIP LU6 .....5...
Pirton Hill Infant School
  LTNW/LEA LU4 .....3...
Pirton Hill Primary School
  LTNW/LEA LU4 .....3...
Premier Travel Inn
  DUN/WHIP LU6 .....5...
  LTNE LU2 .....4...
Priory Middle School
  DUN/WHIP LU6 .....5...
Putteridge High School
  LTNE LU2 .....3...
Putteridge J & I School
  LTNE LU2 .....3...
Pyghtle School
  AMP/FLIT/BLC MK45 .....
Quadrant Shopping Centre
  DUN/WHIP LU6 .....
Queensbury School
  DUN/WHIP LU6 .....
Rabia Girls School
  LTN LU1 .....4...
Ramridge Primary School
  LTNE LU2 .....4...
Ramsey Manor Lower School
  AMP/FLIT/BLC MK45 .....1...
Ravensbury Castle
  HTCH/STOT SG5 .....1...
Redbourn Golf Club
  STALW/RED AL3 .....6...
Redbourn Industrial Centre
  STALW/RED AL3 .....7...
Redbourn J & I School
  STALW/RED AL3 .....7...
Redbourn Recreation Centre
  STALW/RED AL3 .....6...
Richmond Hill Special School
  LTNE LU2 .....
Riverside Estate
  HARP AL5 .....
Roundwood JMI School
  HARP AL5 .....6...
Roundwood Park School
  HARP AL5 .....
Sacred Heart J & I School
  LTNE LU2 .....
St Christophers Lower School
  DUN/HR/TOD LU5 .....
St Dominic RC Primary School
  DUN/HR/TOD LU5 .....
St George of England CP School
  DUN/HR/TOD LU5 .....
St Georges School
  DUN/HR/TOD LU5 .....
St Georges School Technology
  College
  HARP AL5 .....
St Hildas School
  HARP AL5 .....
St Joseph's J & I School
  LTNN/LIM LU3 .....
St Lukes Special School
  STALW/RED AL3 .....7...
St Margaret of Scotland
  Infant School
  LTN LU1 .....
St Martin de Porres Primary
  School *LTNW/LEA* LU4 .....
St Marys Lower School
  LTNE LU2 .....
St Matthews Infant School
  LTNE LU2 .....
St Nicholas Primary School
  HARP AL5 .....
St Vincents Lower School
  DUN/HR/TOD LU5 .....
Sauncey Wood
  Primary School
  HARP AL5 .....

...re School
NW/LEA LU4 ....32 B2
...ght School
...*ALW/RED* AL5 ....60 D5
...ill House Museum
...*ALW/RED* AL3 ....71 E2
...hn Lawes School
...*RP* AL5 ....69 E1
...nd Lower School
...*N* LU1 ....53 H5
...eries Castle
...*NE* LU2 ....56 A1
...eries J & I School
...*NE* LU2 ....45 G1
...h Bedfordshire Golf Club
...*NE* LU2 ....24 B5
...h Bedfordshire
...agistrates Court *LTN* LU1 ......4 B5
...ndown Industrial Estate
...*RP* AL5 ....69 E4
...field J & I School
...*NW/LEA* LU4 ....31 H4
...h Luton High School
...*N* LU1 ....54 D1
...um Industrial Estate
...*NW/LEA* LU4 ....42 B1
...pridge Lower School
...*UZ* LU7 ....28 B3
...wood Craft Museum &
...rdens *LTN* LU1 ....54 B2
...wood Park Athletic Track
...*N* LU1 ....54 B3

Stockwood Park Country Park
  LTN LU1 ....54 B3
Stockwood Park Golf Club
  LTN LU1 ....54 B2
Stopsley High School &
  Community College
  LTNE LU2 ....34 D4
Stopsley Primary School
  LTNE LU2 ....35 E4
Stopsley Sports Centre &
  Sports Ground
  LTNE LU2 ....35 E3
Streetfield Middle School
  DUN/HR/TOD LU5 ....41 G5
Studham Lower School
  LTNN/LIM LU3 ....58 D5
Sundon Business Park
  LTNN/LIM LU3 ....22 B5
Sundon Hills Country Park
  LTNN/LIM LU3 ....14 C4
Sundon Industrial Estate
  LTNN/LIM LU3 ....22 B5
Sundon Lower School
  LTNN/LIM LU3 ....22 B1
Sundon Medical Centre
  LTNN/LIM LU3 ....32 C1
Sundon Park Junior School
  LTNN/LIM LU3 ....22 C5
Surrey Street Primary School
  LTN LU1 ....4 D7
Telmere Industrial Estate
  LTN LU1 ....4 D7

Tennyson Road Primary School
  LTN LU1 ....54 B1
Thames Industrial Estate
  DUN/WHIP LU6 ....2 D5
Thomas Whitehead
  CE School
  DUN/HR/TOD LU5 ....30 D5
Thornhill Lower School
  LTNN/LIM LU3 ....31 F1
Tilsworth Golf Centre
  LBUZ LU7 ....29 F2
Tithe Farm Lower School
  DUN/HR/TOD LU5 ....30 D2
Toddington Health Clinic
  DUN/HR/TOD LU5 ....12 B4
Toddington Medical Centre
  DUN/HR/TOD LU5 ....12 C4
Totternhoe FC
  DUN/WHIP LU6 ....39 G4
Totternhoe Lower School
  DUN/WHIP LU6 ....39 F4
Totternhoe Quarry
  Nature Reserve
  DUN/WHIP LU6 ....39 F3
Townsend Industrial Estate
  DUN/HR/TOD LU5 ....30 D4
Travelodge
  DUN/HR/TOD LU5 ....13 F4
  LBUZ LU7 ....18 D4
  LTNW/LEA LU4 ....42 D1
Tree Cathedral (NT)
  DUN/WHIP LU6 ....50 B5

University of Luton
  LTN LU1 ....4 E5
  LTNE LU2 ....35 H2
The Vale Cemetery
  LTNE LU2 ....35 F2
The Vale Crematorium
  LTNE LU2 ....35 F2
Warden Hill Infant School
  LTNN/LIM LU3 ....34 A1
Warden Hill Junior School
  LTNN/LIM LU3 ....34 A1
Wardown House
  (Luton Museum & Gallery)
  LTNE LU2 ....34 B5
Wardown Swimming &
  Leisure Centre
  LTNN/LIM LU3 ....44 B1
Watling Lower School
  DUN/WHIP LU6 ....2 E7
Waulud Primary School
  LTNN/LIM LU3 ....33 E1
Weatherfield Special School
  DUN/WHIP LU6 ....40 A2
Wenlock Junior School
  LTNE LU2 ....5 J3
Westfield Cemetery *HARP* AL5 ..64 C5
Westoning Lower School
  AMP/FLIT/BLC MK45 ....7 G1
Whipperley Infant School
  LTN LU1 ....43 G5
Whipsnade Park Golf Club
  BERK HP4 ....58 A4

Whipsnade Wild Animal Park
  DUN/WHIP LU6 ....58 B2
Whitefield J & I School
  LTNN/LIM LU3 ....23 E5
White Lion Retail Park
  DUN/HR/TOD LU5 ....3 F2
Wigmore Primary School
  LTNE LU2 ....46 A1
William Austin Infant School
  LTNN/LIM LU3 ....34 A4
William Austin Junior School
  LTNN/LIM LU3 ....34 A4
Willowfield Lower School
  LTN LU1 ....53 F2
Willowgate Trading Estate
  LTNN/LIM LU3 ....22 B5
Windmill Trading Estate
  LTN LU1 ....5 G5
Wood End School
  HARP AL5 ....67 H1
Woodlands Secondary School
  LTNN/LIM LU3 ....33 F1
Woodside Clinic
  DUN/HR/TOD LU5 ....3 G5
Woodside Farm &
  Wildfowl Park
  STALW/RED AL3 ....61 F1
Woodside Industrial Estate
  DUN/HR/TOD LU5 ....31 F5
Woodside Park
  Industrial Estate
  DUN/HR/TOD LU5 ....31 E5

Acknowledgements

...Post Office is a registered trademark of Post Office Ltd. in the UK and other countries.

...ools address data provided by Education Direct.

...ol station information supplied by Johnsons

...way street data provided by © Tele Atlas N.V. Tele Atlas

...en centre information provided by

...en Centre Association   Britains best garden centres

...vale Garden Centres

...statement on the front cover of this atlas is sourced, selected and quoted
  a reader comment and feedback form received in 2004

 **Street by Street** QUESTIONNAIRE

Dear Atlas User
Your comments, opinions and recommendations are very important to us.
So please help us to improve our street atlases by taking a few minutes
to complete this simple questionnaire.

You do not need a stamp (unless posted outside the UK). If you do not want to remove this page from your street atlas, then photocopy it or write your answers on a plain sheet of paper.

Send to: The Editor, AA Street by Street, FREEPOST SCE 4598,
Basingstoke RG21 4GY

ABOUT THE ATLAS...

Which city/town/county did you buy?

Are there any features of the atlas or mapping that you find particularly useful?

Is there anything we could have done better?

Why did you choose an AA Street by Street atlas?

Did it meet your expectations?

Exceeded ☐   **Met all** ☐   **Met most** ☐   **Fell below** ☐

Please give your reasons

continued overleaf

Where did you buy it?

For what purpose? (please tick all applicable)

To use in your own local area ☐   To use on business or at work ☐

Visiting a strange place ☐   In the car ☐   On foot ☐

Other (please state)

LOCAL KNOWLEDGE...

Local knowledge is invaluable. Whilst every attempt has been made to make the information contained in this atlas as accurate as possible, should you notice any inaccuracies, please detail them below (if necessary, use a blank piece of paper) or e-mail us at *streetbystreet@theAA.com*

ABOUT YOU...

Name (Mr/Mrs/Ms)

Address

Postcode

Daytime tel no   **Mobile tel no**

E-mail address

Please only give us your e-mail address and mobile phone number if you wish to hear from us about other products and services from the AA and partners by e-mail or text or mms.

Which age group are you in?

Under 25 ☐   25-34 ☐   35-44 ☐   45-54 ☐   55-64 ☐   65+ ☐

Are you an AA member?   YES ☐   NO ☐

Do you have Internet access?   YES ☐   NO ☐

The information we hold about you will be used to provide the product(s) and service(s) requested and for identification, account administration, analysis, and fraud/loss prevention purposes. More details about how that information is used is in our Privacy Statement, which you will find under the heading "Personal information" in our Terms and Conditions and on our website. Copies are available from us by post, by contacting our Data Protection Manager at AA, Fanum House, Basing View, Hampshire, Basingstoke RG21 4EA.

We may want to contact you about other products and services provided by us or our partners but please tick the box if you DO NOT wish to hear about such products and services from us by mail or telephone. ☐

Thank you for taking the time to complete this questionnaire. Please send it to us as soon as possible, and remember, you do not need a stamp (unless posted outside the UK).   ML107y